EX LIBRIS

Aug. 16, 1956

To Lorry,

May the wisdom and
beauty of this volumn provide
you with many peaceful hours.

Dickie

SAINT FRANCIS AND THE POET

Saint Francis and

the poet

poems on Saint Francis of Assisi
1200 A.D. to the present
edited by Elizabeth B. Patterson
preface by Richard J. Cushing, D.D.
foreword by Fray Angelico Chavez, O.F.M.
decorations by Walter Miles

THE DEVIN-ADAIR COMPANY   NEW YORK   1956

NIHIL OBSTAT
Santa Fe, N. M., March 17, 1956
Rev. George A. Woods, *Censor Librorum*

IMPRIMATUR
Santa Fe, March 19, 1956
✠ Most Rev. Edwin V. Byrne, Archbishop of Santa Fe

© Copyright 1956 by the Devin-Adair Company.

Canadian agents: Thomas Nelson & Sons, Ltd., Toronto.

Library of Congress Catalog Card No.: 56-8129

Designed by Walter Miles.

Manufactured in the United States of America.

Thomas A. Daly; "The Birds and Francis" from *Food and Drink* by Louis Untermeyer, copyright 1935 by Harcourt, Brace and Co.

Harper and Brothers for "St. Francis Weds the Three Maidens" from *Balm in Gilead* by Helene Mullins, copyright 1930 by Harper and Brothers.

The New York *Herald Tribune* for "To Saint Francis" by A. Babington Smith. New York *Herald Tribune* and Frances Frost for "Prayer to St. Francis" by Frances Frost.

Houghton Mifflin Co. for "Saint Francis Endeth His Sermon" from *Happy Ending* by Louise Imogen Guiney; "At Assisi" from *The Collected Poems of William Vaughn Moody*.

Bruce Humphries, Inc., for "Saint Francis" from *Afternoons in Eden* by Amanda Benjamin Hall.

John Lane, The Bodley Head, Ltd., for "A Franciscan Dream," "A Franciscan Prayer," and "The Mendicant" by Enid Dinnis; "Saint Francis to the Birds" by Katharine Tynan Hinkson; "The Singing Saint" by J. B. Morton; "The Irish Franciscan" by Rosa Mulholland; and "Mount Avernia" by H. E. G. Rope from *Louis Vincent's Anthology of Franciscan Poetry and Prose*.

J. B. Lippincott Co. for "Assisi" and "The Nestling Church at Ovingdean" by Alfred Noyes.

Longmans, Green and Co. for "Music" from *God's Ambuscade* by Daniel Sargent.

The Macmillan Co. for "Cloister" from *Cloister and Other Poems* by Charles L. O'Donnell, C.S.C.

The Macmillan Co. of Canada, Ltd., for "The Blessing of Saint Francis" from *Franciscan Rimes for Children* by Sister Maura.

Virgil Markham for special permission to use the poem "To Saint Francis" from *Collected Poems* by Edwin Markham, published by Doubleday, Doran.

Oxford University Press, Inc., for "A Rhyme for Francis: October 4th" from *Ten Saints* by Eleanor Farjeon, copyright 1936 by Oxford University Press, Inc.

The Poor Clare Sisters, Bordentown, N.J., for "Saint Francis' Lesson to His Brothers" by a Sister of the Poor Clares.

The Poor Clare Sisters, Roswell, N. M., for "Children of Francis: 1953," "Epitaph," "Genealogy," and "Memorandum to St. Francis—April 16" by Sister Mary Francis, P.C.

G. P. Putnam's Sons for "Saint Francis" from *Tree of Time* by Gertrude Huntington McGiffert.

Rinehart and Co., Inc., for "The Roses of Saint Francis" from *Shadow of the Perfect Rose* by Thomas S. Jones, Jr., edited by John L. Foley, copyright 1937 by John L. Foley.

Saint Anthony Guild for "Saint Francis to the Birds" by Clement Cook, O.F.M.

Saint Anthony Messenger for "Prayer to St. Francis for Poverty" by Liam Brophy; "St. Francis of Assisi" by Harry F. Leary.

The Sign for "The Rich Man of Assisi" by Sister M. Benvenuta.

The Sisters of the Holy Cross Order for "The Vocation of St. Francis" by Sister Eleanore, C.S.C.; "Spendthrift" by Sister M. Genoveva, C.S.C.; "I Go to School," "Roses for My King," "Things to Be Loved" by Sister M. Madeleva, C.S.C.; "The Wolf of Gubbio Speaks to Saint Francis" by Sister Mary Monica, C.S.C.

Spirit for "Marionette" by Fray Angelico Chavez, copyright by The Catholic Poetry Society of America.

Sunward (Oglethorpe University Press) for "Saint Francis of Assisi" by Tom Sweeney.

PREFACE

From every possible point of view it can be asserted that the appeal of Saint Francis of Assisi is both universal and compelling. Il Poverello has been acclaimed by philosophers and statesmen, by artists and artisans, by those who are confirmed in the faith and by those who have known no faith, by those who revel in the delights of the present and by those who mourn here below that they may be comforted hereafter.

My own interest in Saint Francis is that of one who has found in him a source of inspiration for the active life of a diocesan pastor of souls. A priest, and more especially a bishop, must learn to be detached from the world, while living in it. He must see in his people the image of their Creator without losing the human touch that will keep him in close contact with them. He must be cheerful in adversity. He must find his greatest joy in the discharge of his priestly duties. He must have a single-hearted devotion to the cause of Christ and His Church. In a word, he must reflect in every phase of his ministry the spirit of Saint Francis, who loved the world because he loved God, and who was supremely happy in the world because he saw in every corner of it the infinite beauty of its Creator.

I am happy to contribute to the success which Mrs. Patterson's anthology deserves by my own word of commendation and encouragement. I rejoice that Saint Francis, for whom I have cherished a special devotion through all the years of my service in Christ's Church, will become better known and appreciated by all who will read and meditate on the carefully selected passages which this book presents in such attractive form. After all, the life of Saint Francis is but the life of Christ. No one can become a true son of Saint Francis without mirroring more accurately in his own life the divine perfection of Him Who took upon Himself our humanity that He might make each one of us a sharer in the Nature which He shared with His Father and the Holy Ghost. May St. Francis, whose praises are sung in this book in the inspired language of poetry by so many of those who have followed his way of spiritual life, impart his heavenly blessing on all who are reached by its message and will thus be brought into closer union with Christ our Lord.

✠ RICHARD J. CUSHING, D.D.

Archbishop's Residence
Boston, Mass.

FOREWORD

Good St. Francis of Assisi, from that golden dusk when the larks sang at his passing seven hundred and more years ago down to our less halcyon nuclear day, has in every period attracted the artist and the dilettante, the poet and the poetaster, to such an extent that one might well imagine the gentle Saint throwing up his pierced hands and calling a halt to all the painting and the rhyming. This he would have done during his lifetime, out of pure humility, not from any disdain for his vast and odd army of admirers in every age. But I am sure that from heaven he embraces all the painters and singers alike, drawing no lines of distinction between the famed masters of their particular art and the less-gifted wooers of the Muses.

With regard to lyric poetry especially, the author and singer of "The Canticle of Creatures" must rejoice at all the poems about himself that are forever sprouting, and which he in turn hands over in spiritual bouquets to the Lord, since anyone who sings about Francis must, in some way, remember and praise God. In brief, the *Little Flowers* of St. Francis prove to be a veritable perennial garden of delight which inspires new species, and where the humblest flower is welcome to grow for a greater Glory.

This is not to say that the poems in this collection are to be divided into masterpieces and doggerel. But there is a distinction among them, between the selections that reach, or those that almost reach, the very heights of poetry, and those that have merely attained to excellence in verse. Yet, here all grow well together. An anthology, literally, is a garden of word flowers, and a Franciscan anthology need not be all roses—rather, a varied garden of flowers, so long as they are really flowers, where the daisy and dahlia praise God in the same patch of sunlight.

Here, too, lies the answer to those who may ask: "Why another anthology on St. Francis?" Old collections of poetry tend to go to seed; they finally go out of print or are forgotten. Old flower plants have to be taken up, re-sorted, new beds must be made. Some plants are discarded because better ones of the genus or species have been developed. But there is always that dependable background of hardy perennials that never die or which cannot be improved upon, the poetry of the masters. And once again the season is beautified with a remade garth of seraphic flowers, the old and the new, the rare and resplendent as well as the humble but ever charming.

May this current season's garden be the delight of every lover of the *Fioretti,* as it will surely please the gentle Bard of Assisi, the more so if the reader, in admiring the hues and inhaling the fragrance, gives praise to Him Who made us all and every good thing.

FR. ANGELICO CHAVEZ, O.F.M.

Santa Fe, New Mexico

CONTENTS

ACKNOWLEDGMENTS

I wish to give grateful acknowledgment to the following persons who have contributed not only selections for inclusion in this volume, but also valuable research material relating to it:

Mother Francis d'Assisi, O.S.U., Sister M. Margaret Patricia, Sister Agnes Lucile, S.P., Leonard Mahoney, S.J., Edward F. Garesché, S.J., Terence L. Connolly, S.J., Marion A. Habig, O.F.M., Hyacinth Blocker, O.F.M., T. F. Kramer, C.PP.S., Fr. Thomas Grassman, O.F.M. Conv., Fr. Mark Hegener, O.F.M., Fr. Norbert F. Lehr, O.F.M., Fr. Alexander Wyse, O.F.M., Katherine Brégy, Elizabeth Morrow, Louisa Boyd Gile, Ethel D. W. Collins, Alma L. Gray, Blanche Mary Kelly, Freda Dewson and the many others not listed.

I have been unable to contact certain few authors whose works are included in this collection. To these also I wish to extend my sincere thanks.

For advice and helpful suggestions in the collection and preparation of this material, I am glad to acknowledge the invaluable assistance given me by my husband, Robert M. Patterson, and my sister, Helen Cassidy.

E. B. P.

INTRODUCTION

Saint Francis of Assisi is described by Gilbert K. Chesterton as a "lean and lively little man, thin as a thread and vibrant as a bowstring." Alfred Lord Tennyson writes, "Sweet Saint Francis of Assisi, would that he were here again." Vachel Lindsay, in his urgent plea for the return of Franciscan ideals, simplicity, and peace, says, "Would I might wake Saint Francis in you all."

This collection of poems is an attempt to retell, in the words of those who have most deeply sensed his spirit, the story of the sandal-footed Troubadour of God. Writers of almost all creeds have sung his praise in verse, and if all the poems in English alone had been included, this work would have become a ponderous volume.

The Little Poor Man of Assisi was a many-sided personality. In these poems he is named saint, ascetic, companion, poet, humanitarian, burning preacher, stigmatic, penitent, singer, and lover of God. He has been all things to all men, yet there never lived a more perfectly integrated person. He was united in himself and to God, a cosmic individualist who was a "mirror of the world."

Saint Francis was born Francesco di Bernardone in 1181 of French-Italian parentage and died in 1226. He compounded earthy Umbrian realism with Provençal sensibilities, austerity with merriment, suffering with song. He was mystic, humanist, poet, both before and after his conversion from worldly life to spiritual. Always the *"joculator,"* he received the imprint of the five wounds and died a stigmatic *"joculator Dei."* He composed and sang "The Canticle of Creatures" in his last illness. When told he was dying, he gratefully added the last lines of the Canticle, wherein he praises Little Sister Death. The many aspects of his life and death are reflected in this book much as they are set down by Saint Bonaventure in his *Life of Saint Francis,* written sometime between 1260 and 1263 A.D.:

Now the beginning of the life of Francis, its course, and its consummation are divided into fifteen chapters, as set down below, and thuswise described:

The first treateth of his manner of life in the secular state.

The second, of his perfect conversion unto God and of the repairing of the three churches.

The third, of the founding of his Religion, and sanction of the Rule.

The fourth, of the advancement of the Order under his hand, and of the confirmation of the Rule already sanctioned.

The fifth, of the austerity of his life, and of how all created things afforded him comfort.

The sixth, of his humility and obedience, and of the divine condescensions shown unto him at will.

The seventh, of his love for Poverty, and of the wondrous supplying of his needs.

The eighth, of the kindly impulses of his piety, and of how the creatures lacking understanding seemed to be made subject unto him.

The ninth, of his ardent love, and yearning for martyrdom.

The tenth, of his zeal and efficacy in prayer.

The eleventh, of his understanding of the Scriptures, and of his spirit of prophecy.

The twelfth, of the efficacy of his preaching, and of his gift of healing.

The thirteenth, of the sacred stigmata.

The fourteenth, of his sufferings and death.

The fifteenth, of his canonization, and the translation of his body.

Thereafter is added some account of the miracles shown after his departure.

Despite its shortcomings, may this collection of verses on Saint Francis of Assisi be in some small way worthy of its subject. And may it be proof that his spirit of peace, humility, and simplicity is today needed more than ever by men of good will.

ELIZABETH B. PATTERSON

Santa Fe, New Mexico, 1956

The Blessing of Saint Francis

Saint Francis of Assisi

May the Lord bless thee
and keep thee;
May He show His face to thee
and have mercy upon thee;
May He turn His countenance
to thee, and give thee peace.
May the Lord bless thee:
Amen.

Prayer for Peace

Saint Francis of Assisi

Lord, make me an instrument of Your Peace.
Where there is hatred, let me sow love;
Where there is injury, pardon;
Where there is doubt, faith;
Where there is despair, hope;
Where there is darkness, light;
And where there is sickness, joy.
O Divine Master, grant that I may not
So much seek to be consoled as to console;
To be understood as to understand;
To be loved as to love;
For it is in giving that we receive;
It is in pardoning that we are pardoned;
And it is in dying
That we are born to eternal life.
    Amen.

Of Order in Our Lord Christ

Saint Francis of Assisi
From the Italian by Dante Gabriel Rossetti

Set love in order, thou that lovest Me,
   Never was virtue out of order found;
And though I fill thy heart desirously,
   By thine own virtue I must keep My ground;
When to My love thou dost bring charity,
   Even she must come with order girt and gowned.
   Look how the trees are bound
To order, bearing fruit;
And by one thing compute
In all things earthly order's grace and gain.

All earthly things I had the making of
   Were numbered and were measured then by Me;
And each was ordered to its end by Love,
   Each kept, through order, clean for ministry.
Charity most of all, when known enough,
   Is of her very nature orderly.
   Lo, now! what heat in thee,
Soul, can have bred this rout?
Thou put'st all order out,
Even this love's heat must be its curb and rein.

Saint Francis' Salute to Our Lady

Saint Francis of Assisi
From the Latin by Marion A. Habig, O.F.M.

Hail, most holy Queen and Lady,
Mary, Mother of Our Lord,
Who a Virgin art forever,
Chosen by the Father's word.

Thee He consecrated wholly
With His loved and holy One,
And the Paraclete, the Spirit,
As the Mother of His Son.

Thine the fulness of all graces;
Thou, His palace home most sweet.
Hail! His Tabernacle, Garment,
Maid and Mother—thee we greet.

The Canticle of Creatures

Saint Francis of Assisi
From the Italian by Marian Douglas, O.F.M.

Most High, Omnipotent, Good Lord,
To You be all praise, glory, honor and benediction.

To You alone, O God Most High, do they belong,
And there is no one worthy to mention Your Name.

Praised be You, my Lord, by means of all Your
    creatures,
And most especially through noble Brother Sun,
Who makes the day, and illumines us by his light.

And he is beautiful and radiant with great splendor;
For he is a symbol of Thee, O God Most High.

Praised be You, my Lord, through Sister Moon and all
    the stars:
For in heaven You have formed them, clear, precious
    and fair.

Praised be You, my Lord, by Brother Wind,
And by the air, the Clouds and Clear Sky and by every

kind of Weather,
Through whom You give to Your creatures
nourishment.

Praised be You, my Lord, through Sister Water,
For she is very useful, humble, precious and chaste.

Praised be You, my Lord, through Brother Fire,
By whom You illumine the night:
For he is gay, mighty and strong.

Praised be You, my Lord, by our Sister Mother Earth,
Who sustains us and keeps us,
And brings forth various fruits along with colored
flowers and leaves.

Praised be You, my Lord, through those who give
pardon because of Your love
And who suffer infirmity and tribulation.

Blessed are they who endure all in peace,
For they, O God Most High, will be crowned by You.

Praised be You, my Lord, through our Sister Bodily
Death,
From whom no living person can escape.

6

Woe to those who die in mortal sin!
But blessed are those found in Your most holy Will,
For the second death will do them no harm.

Praise and bless the Lord,
And thank Him and serve Him with great humility.

Of Holy Poverty

Fra Jacopone da Todi
From the Italian by Mrs. Theodore Beck

O amor de povertate,
Regno de tranquillitate!

Poverty, whose path is safe and clear,
Hath no griefs, nor rancour, sheds no tear,
Nor of robber hands hath any fear,
Tempests cannot trouble Poverty.

Poverty can die in perfect peace;
Maketh neither will, nor bond, nor lease,
Leaves the world behind, and lies at ease,
And around her strife can never be.

Poverty, High Wisdom deep and sure,
Unsubdued by earth and earthly lure,
Scorns created things, detached and pure,
Scorning, yet possessing utterly.

Who despiseth, surely doth possess,
Owning all things without bitterness:
Nothing trips him up, his feet can press
On their daily journey faithfully.

He, whose wants are master, is a slave,
Sells himself for what his longings crave,
Him his purchased riches cannot save;
He hath bargained very foolishly.

Mortal courage sure must hesitate,
Think and turn from such a vassal state,
Where God's image, beautiful and great,
Is debased and changed to vanity.

In a narrow heart God cannot bide;
Where love is great, the heart is wide;
Poverty, great-hearted, dignified,
Entertains and welcomes Deity.

Ah! Where Christ is grafted on the spray,
All the withered wood is cut away;
See, the freshness spring from decay!
Changing to a wondrous Unity.

Love that lives and breathes without Desire,
Wisdom, freed from Thought's consuming fire;
Will, at one with God, that doth aspire
But to obey Him in simplicity. . . .

From The Divine Comedy

Dante Alighieri

From the Italian by Henry F. Cary

But not to deal
Thus closely with thee longer, take at large
The lovers' titles—Poverty and Francis.
Their concord and glad looks, wonder and love,
And sweet regard gave birth to holy thoughts,
So much, that venerable Bernard first
Did bare his feet, and, in pursuit of peace
So heavenly, ran, yet deem'd his footing slow.
O hidden riches! O prolific good!
Egidius bares him next, and next Sylvester,
And follow both the bridegroom; so the bride
Can please them. Thenceforth goes he on his way,
The father and the master, with his spouse,
And with that family, whom now the cord
Girt humbly: nor did abjectness of heart
Weigh down his eyelids, for that he was son
Of Pietro Bernardone, and by men
In wond'rous sort despis'd. But royally
His hard intention he to Innocent
Set forth, and from him first receiv'd the seal
On his religion. Then, when numerous flock'd

10

The tribe of lowly ones, that trac'd *his* steps,
Whose marvellous life deservedly were sung
In heights empyreal, through Honorius' hand
A second crown, to deck their Guardian's virtues,
Was by th' eternal Spirit inwreath'd: and when
He had, through thirst of martyrdom, stood up
In the proud Soldan's presence, and there preach'd
Christ and his followers; but found the race
Unripen'd for conversion: back once more
He hasted (not to intermit his toil),
And reap'd Ausonian lands. On the hard rock,
'Twixt Arno and the Tiber, he from Christ
Took the last signet, which his limbs two years
Did carry. Then the season come, that he,
Who to such good had destin'd him, was pleas'd
T' advance him to the meed, which he had earn'd
By his self-humbling, to his brotherhood,
As their just heritage, he gave in charge
His dearest lady, and enjoin'd their love
And faith to her: and, from her bosom, will'd
His goodly spirit should move forth, returning
To its appointed kingdom, nor would have
His body laid upon another bier.

Love's Franciscan

Sweet hand! the sweet yet cruel bow thou art,
From whence at one, five ivory arrows fly,
So with five wounds at once I wounded lie
Bearing in breast the print of every dart.
Saint Francis had the like, yet felt no smart:
Where I in living torments never die,
His wounds were in his hands and feet where I
All these same helpless wounds feel in my heart.
Now as Saint Francis (if a saint) am I.
The bow which shot these shafts a relic is;
I mean the hand, which is the reason why
So many for devotion thee would kiss,
And I thy glove kiss as a thing divine;
Thy arrows quiver, and thy relics shine.

The Friar

Julian del Casal

From the Spanish by Thomas Walsh

Barefooted, in his hood and cloak of brown,
   Mounted upon his burro's chubby back
   To beg the pious alms that fill his sack
The old Franciscan starts at dawn for town.
Behind him sounds the early belfry down
   To call to Mass the faithful in his track;
   The summons floats afar into the wrack
Of pink and golden clouds, the dawning's crown.

His breviary at his elbow tucked away,
His rosary rattling heavily with his sway,
   He reckons that his givers shall not lag;
And hearkens as he paces down the road,
Between the burro's braying for the load,
   The wind that whistles through his empty bag.

From The Cuckoo at Laverna

William Wordsworth

Oft have I heard the Nightingale and Thrush
Blending as in a common English grove
Their love-songs; but, where'er my feet might roam,
Whate'er assemblages of new and old,
Strange and familiar, might beguile the way,
A gratulation from that vagrant voice
Was wanting;—and most happily till now.

  For see, Laverna! mark the far-famed Pile,
High on the brink of that precipitous rock,
Implanted like a Fortress, as in truth
It is, a Christian Fortress, garrisoned
In faith and hope, and dutiful obedience,
By a few Monks, a stern society,
Dead to the world and scorning earth-born joys.
Nay—though the hopes that drew, the fears that
      drove
St. Francis, far from Man's resort, to abide
Among these sterile heights of Apennine,
Bound him, nor, since he raised yon House, have
      ceased
To bind his spiritual Progeny, with rules
Stringent as flesh can tolerate and live;

His milder Genius (thanks to the good God
That made us) over those severe restraints
Of mind, that dread heart-freezing discipline,
Doth sometimes here predominate, and works
By unsought means for gracious purposes;
For earth through heaven, for heaven, by changeful
    earth,
Illustrated, and mutually endeared.

    Rapt though he were above the power of sense,
Familiarly, yet out of the cleansed heart
Of that once sinful being overflowed
On sun, moon, stars, the nether elements,
And every shape of creature they sustain,
Divine affections; and with beast and birds,
(Stilled from afar—such marvel story tells—
By casual outbreak of his passionate words,
And from their own pursuits in field or grove
Drawn to his side by look or act of love
Humane, and virtue of his innocent life)
He wont to hold companionship so free,
So pure, so fraught with knowledge and delight
As to be likened in his followers' minds
To that which our first Parents, ere the fall
From their high state darkened the Earth with fear,
Held with all Kinds in Eden's blissful bowers.

Saint Francis' Sermon to the Birds

Henry W. Longfellow

Up soared the lark into the air,
A shaft of song, a wingèd prayer,
As if a soul, released from pain,
Were flying back to heaven again.

Saint Francis heard; it was to him
An emblem of the Seraphim;
The upward motion of the fire,
The light, the heat, the heart's desire.

Around Assisi's convent gate
The birds, the poor who cannot wait,
From moor and mere and darksome wood
Came flocking for their dole of food.

"O brother birds," St. Francis said,
"Ye come to me and ask for bread,
But not with bread alone today
Shall ye be fed and sent away.

"Ye shall be fed, ye happy birds,
With manna of celestial words;
Not mine, though mine they seem to be,
Not mine, though they be spoken through me.

"O, doubly are ye bound to praise
The great Creator in your lays;
He giveth you your plumes of down
Your crimson hoods, your cloaks of brown.

"He giveth you your wings to fly
And breathe a purer air on high,
And careth for you everywhere,
Who for yourselves so little care!"

With flutter of swift wings and songs
Together rose the feathered throngs,
And singing scattered far apart;
Deep peace was in St. Francis' heart.

He knew not if the brotherhood
His homily had understood;
He only knew that to one ear
The meaning of his words was clear.

Mount Alvernia

H. E. G. Rope

A dark blue crest in the azure skies,
  The long, brown slopes below—
Unto the hill lift up thine eyes,
  Lift up thy heart also.
Dark-crown'd, outstanding
  Aloof, commanding
    La Verna.

Over the world it stands enthroned,
  It stands, Heaven's own watch-tower,
Over the world and its ways disowned,
  Over the clamant hour.
A stronghold dark,
  A refuge-ark,
    La Verna.

Legate of Heaven and interceder,
  Lover of souls and friend,
Giver of grace to every needer,
  Chanting the chant without end,
A treasure city
  Of love and pity,
    La Verna.

Crown'd with many a cross, and chiming
   With benison of bells
Up through the mystic forest climbing,
   Down-floating o'er the fells,
Enwall me and hold me,
      La Verna.

Saint Francis

Alfred Lord Tennyson

. . . Are we devils? Are we men?
Sweet Saint Francis of Assisi,
Would that he were here again,
He who in his catholic wholeness
Called the very birds and flowers
Brothers, sisters.

The Irish Franciscan

Rosa Mulholland (Lady Gilbert)

A barefoot friar all in brown,
Weather-beat face and storm-rent gown,
Tattered hood over shaven crown,
Travelled as the sun goes down.

Whither ere morning goeth he
Over the bog he moveth free;
Bog so brown it were hard to see
That brown man travelling patiently.

Hidden under his threadbare vest
He holdeth One close to his breast:
"O Lord, in what poor place of rest
This winter's eve thou harbourest!"

Deep in the pools the red lights die,
Darkness veileth the western sky;
Only the plovers cry and cry
"Amen" to prayers as they flitter by.

Who are these, thou barefoot man,
Weak and weary and under a ban,
Who meet thee in the starlight wan?
Columb, and Patrick, and Adamnan!

Three with torches faint and white,
Threading the holes to give thee light,
Bowing before the One of might
Thou bearest with thee through the night.

Now the dawn opens in the east,
There's the altar, and here the priest;
Welcome now to the last and least,
Who hunger for the Master's feast.

Table of rock, and cloth of moss
(Gold and silver are Mammon's dross),
Rude is the stone, and rude the cross,
O Christ our gain, O World our loss!

Ye banned and outlawed of the faith!
Shrive ye now with bated breath;
Hither the hunter hasteneth,
Fear not the little pain of death.

Shines the moon on the curling sea,
Sighs the wind in the white-thorn tree;
Forth from the bough as the gale blows free
Swingeth a figure dolorously.

A barefoot friar all in brown,
Weather-beat face and threadbare gown,
Girdle of rope and shaven crown—
Swingeth he as the moon goes down.

The Lady Poverty

Alice Meynell

The Lady Poverty was fair:
But she has lost her looks of late,
With change of times and change of air.
Ah slattern! she neglects her hair,
Her gown, her shoes; she keeps no state
As once when her pure feet were bare.

Or—almost worse, if worse can be—
She scolds in parlours, dusts and trims,
Watches and counts. Oh, is this she
Whom Francis met, whose step was free,
Who with Obedience carolled hymns,
In Umbria walked with Chastity?

Where is her ladyhood? Not here,
Not among modern kinds of men;
But in the stony fields, where clear
Through the thin trees the skies appear,
In delicate spare soil and fen,
And slender landscape and austere.

The Wagon of the Little Sisters

Hugh Francis Blunt

Milord Saint Francis wed today;
   I saw his carriage pass;
The bride was dressed in strange array,—
   She was no comely lass.

The carriage was no pretty thing
   ('Twas very like a hearse)
But yet she proudly bore his ring,
   For better or for worse.

A "Little Sister of the Poor"—
   The only name had she;
But Francis led her to God's door
   As *Lady* Poverty.

Brother Ass and Saint Francis

John Banister Tabb

It came to pass
That "Brother Ass"
(As he his Body named),
Unto the Saint
Thus made complaint:
"I am unjustly blamed.

"Whate'er I do,
Like Balaam you
Requite me with a blow,
As for offense
To recompense
An ignominious foe.

"God made us one,
And I have done
No wickedness alone;
Nor can I do
Apart, as you,
An evil all my own.

"If Passion stir,
'Tis you that spur
My frenzy to the goal;
Then be the blame
Where sits the shame,
Upon the goading soul.

"Should one or both
Be blind or loth
Our brotherhood to see,
Remember this,
You needs must miss
Or enter heaven through *me.*"

To this complaint
The lowly saint
In tears replied, "Alas,
If so it be,
God punish me
And bless thee, Brother Ass."

The Singing Saint

J. B. Morton

St. Francis walked in Umbria
Seven hundred years ago;
His soul was gladdened at the sight
Of those strong hills, where all the night
The fireflies dance, and silver light
Gleams where the olives grow.

With lowly men in Umbria
He sang the sweet refrains
Of Southern songs that lift the heart,
He preached the Faith in Church and mart,
Until the skies were torn apart,
And Christ walked in the plains.

The little man of Umbria
He praised with all his might
The Lord who made the little things,
Who fashioned birds with beating wings,
And slaked the earth with water-springs,
And dowered with stars the night.

26

The faith he found in Umbria
He taught it to the throng;
For emblem of the Faith he took
Not lowered eyes and solemn look,
Nor frozen heart, nor printed book,
But laughter and loud song.

Portrait

Máire Cotter

With tonsured hair and figure spare
  (Disturbing to the proud),
His sandalled feet the dust may greet,
  His garb is also shroud.

Franciscus Christificatus

Francis Thompson

Thief that has leaped Heaven's star-spiked wall!
Christ's exultant bacchanal!
Wine-smears on thy hand and foot
Of the Vine that struck its root
Deep in Virgin soul, and was
Trained against the reared Cross:
Nay, thy very side its stain
Hath, to make it redly plain
How in the wassail quaffed full part
That flown vintager, thy heart.
Christ in blood stamps Himself afresh
On thy Veronical-veil of flesh.

Lovers, looking with amaze on
Each other, would be that they gaze on:
So for man's love God would be
Man, and man for His love He:
What God in Christ, man has in thee.
God gazed on man and grew embodied,
Thou, on Him gazing, turn'st engodded!
But though He held thy brow-spread tent
His little Heaven above Him bent,

The scept'ring reed suffices thee,
Which smote Him into sovereignty.

Thou who thoughtest thee too low
For His priest, thou shalt not so
'Scape Him and unpriested go!
In thy hand thou wouldst not hold Him,
In thy flesh thou shalt enfold Him;
Bread wouldst not change into Him . . . ah see!
How He doth change Himself to thee!

Saint Francis to the Birds

Katharine Tynan Hinkson

Little sisters, the birds:
  We must praise God, you and I—
  You, with songs that fill the sky,
I, with halting words.

All things tell His praise,
  Woods and waters thereof sing,
  Summer, Winter, Autumn, Spring,
And the nights and days.

Yea, and cold and heat,
  And the sun and stars and moon,
  Sea with her monotonous tune,
Rain and hail and sleet.

And the winds of heaven,
  And the solemn hills of blue,
  And the brown earth and the dew,
And the thunder even.

And the flowers' sweet breath.
   All things make one glorious voice;
   Life with fleeting pains and joys,
And our Sister, Death.

Little flowers of air,
   With your feathers soft and sleek
   And your brightest eyes and meek,
He hath made you fair.

He hath taught to you
   Skill to weave in tree and thatch
   Nests where happy mothers hatch
Speckled eggs of blue,

And hath children given.
   When the soft heads overbrim
   The brown nests, then thank ye Him
In the clouds of heaven.

Also in your lives
   Live His laws Who loveth you.
   Husbands, be ye kind and true;
Be home-keeping, wives—

Love not gossiping;
    Stay at home and keep the nest;
    Fly not here and there in quest
Of the newest thing.

Live as brethren live:
    Love be in each heart and mouth;
    Be not envious, be not wroth,
Be not slow to give.

When ye build the nest,
    Quarrel not o'er straw or wool;
    He hath been bountiful
To the neediest.

Be not puffed nor vain
    Of your beauty or your worth,
    Of your children or your birth,
Or the praise you gain.

Eat not greedily:
    Sometimes, for sweet mercy's sake,
    Worm or insect spare to take;
Let it crawl or fly.

See ye sing not near
  To our church on holy day,
  Lest the human-folk should stray
From their prayers to hear.

Now depart in peace:
  In God's name I bless each one;
  May your days be long i' the sun
And your joys increase.

And remember me,
  Poor Brother Francis, who
  Loves you, and gives thanks to you
For this courtesy.

Sometimes when ye sing,
  Name my name, that He may take
  Pity for the dear song's sake
On my shortcoming.

A Franciscan Dream

Enid Dinnis

Sweet and clean and dainty,
So may she come to me—
Dainty and sweet, on her naked feet,
The Lady Poverty.

A three-roomed cot and a garden plot
For the beasts and the birds and me,
I ask of her, clean and dainty,
The Lady Poverty.

A mug and a bowl and a platter,
And a cup for the passing guest,
A board of deal for the evening meal
At a casement looking west
(At the sunlit goal of the Quest).
A starlit Room for slumber
When I flee to the land of Nod—
No curtain drawn to hide the dawn,
And a window giving on God.
(Far o'er the hills untrod.)

Christ—on His Cross above me,
To make the white walls fair;
Our Lady's face to gain me grace,
And an image of sweet Saint Claire.

Dainty and meek and holy,
So shall she come to me,
In russet gown, with her eyes cast down,
The Lady Poverty.

And a guest room for the Christ Child
When all the inns are shut—
To rest His limb, and shelter Him,
A hut beside my hut.
Loving and kind and tender,
So shall she come to me
With food for two the whole year through,
The Lady Poverty.

Teapot brew and porridge,
And whatever the good God send,
A log ablaze on winter days
For me and my four-foot friend
(And whomever the good God send).

Books on a shelf beside me
To lift my soul from earth—
A book of prayer and a book of praise,
And a little book of mirth.

Flowers to deck my garden,
These shall my Lady bring,
Strewing her rosy riches,
And her lilies clad like a king,
And a cabbage patch shall she vote me,
And a spade to turn the clod,
And Francis bless my handiness
With a dream of the Garden of God.
With a tool and a book and a platter,
So be my Lady sent;
So shall she scheme with a task and a dream,
The joy of a full content.
Tender and sweet and dainty,
So may she come to me,
In humble guise, with her starry eyes,
The Lady Poverty.

A Franciscan Prayer

Enid Dinnis

When I am old and tutored by
   The grim experience of days;
   When I have proved men in their ways,
Oh, do not let the dreamer die.

When I have learned aside to toss
   The foolish things that wise men hate,
   Lest Littleness should hold me great,
Be mine the folly of the Cross.

When comes detachment's strength to me,
   Let mine the weakness be that wept
   O'er Lazarus's grave and kept
Three comrades in Gethsemane.

When head bids heart herself forget,
   When Reason's lure would love deceive,
   May my poor foolish heart achieve
A few life-giving blunders yet.

When I have grown too sane, too sad,
   To join the angels' faerie ring
   And serve the play-time of the King,
Then, Sweet Saint Francis, make me mad.

The Mendicant

Enid Dinnis

A ghostly rogue and vagabond
I foot the upland track,
Nor bide behind one cloister wall
But beg an alms of each and all
To carry in my pack.

My habit 'tis the beggar's cloak
Whereat men merry make—
A patch of gray, a patch of brown,
The motley of a monarch's clown
Worn gaily for His sake.

Of Benedict his sons I beg
A maxim for my day.
Where Carmel sounds her stintless psalms
I crave a spiritual alms
To sing me on my way.

At sweet St. Brigid's board I'm fed
When on her door I knock;
I share the Servites' broken bread,
And find a pillow for my head
Where Philip folds his flock.

38

Ignatius speeds me on my road
With nectar from his bowl,
The cheer of Bernard wings my feet
And Dominic and Francis meet
And mingle in their dole.

To beg my spirit's livelihood
I've paused at every gate—
At every hostel of the Rood
As "Brother Nobody" pursued
My soul's novitiate.

And now, when these my motley rags
The passing pilgrims scan,
Whate'er their scrip, whate'er their sign,
Their hearts cry gladly, greeting mine,
"Hail! Brother Everyman!"

At Assisi

William Vaughn Moody

Before St. Francis' burg I wait,
Frozen in spirit, faint with dread;
His presence stands within the gate,
Mild splendor rings his head.
Gently he seems to welcome me:
Know he not I am quick, and he
Is dead, and priest of the dead?

I turn away from the gray church pile;
I dare not enter, thus undone:
Here in the roadside grass awhile
I will lie and watch for the sun.
Too purged of earth's good glee and strife,
Too drained of the honeyed lusts of life
Was the peace these old saints won!

And lo! how the laughing earth says no.
To the fear that mastered me;
To the blood that aches and clamors so
How it whispers "Verily."
Here by my side, marvellous-dyed,
Bold stray-away from the courts of pride,
A poppy-bell flaunts free.

St. Francis sleeps upon his hill,
And a poppy-flower laughs down his creed;
Triumphant light her petals spill,
His shrines are dim indeed.
Men build and plan, but the soul of man,
Coming with haughty eyes to scan,
Feels richer, wilder need.

How long, old builder Time, wilt bide
Till, at thy thrilling word,
Life's crimson pride shall have to bride
The spirit's white accord,
Within that gate of good estate
Which thou must build us soon or late,
Hoar workman of the Lord?

The Vocation of St. Francis

Sister Eleanore, C.S.C.

Oh, a leper must be a terrible thing to see
When one is beautiful, young, and free!

Young Francis went out riding, upon a summer's day;
His horse was nobly handsome, and his clothes were
   richly gay.
Suddenly coming toward him upon the road he saw
A leper. He halted his horse and watched the figure
   draw
Nearer and nearer, pale and horrible in the light.
Francis had never known fear before, but now he
   sensed its might—
For a leper is such a terrible thing to see
When one is beautiful, young, and free.
There is something gallantly great in the banners of
   a foe,
And the glory of arms and trumpets all soldiers know.
But fear was born within and came out from Francis'
   heart
To stand there on the road, a cursèd thing apart
From human ways. Then Francis sprang to the
   ground.

42

He ran to the shrinking leper and threw his arms
    around
His fear, holding it to his brave, young breast—
The queens of Assisi's beauty his arms might have
    caressed!
He gave the leper money and kissed him and rode
    on—
But when he turned to wave farewell, lo, the leper
    was gone!
Then Francis knew by the brighter sunlight on the
    dust
That all the poor brothers of Christ were given him
    in trust.

Oh, a leper may be a glorious thing to see
When one is beautiful, young, and free!

To Saint Francis

*(On the occasion of the celebration
of his seventh centenary)*

Edwin Markham

O Francis, doer of lovely things,
All Italy with your spirit sings.
You gentled wolves, communed with birds,
Were friend of all the flocks and herds.
You found a Sister in the stream,
A Brother in the sun's soft beam.
Your glowing heart went out to all
In humble hut or lordly hall.

In what things were you richest, pray?
Only in those you gave away.
But ah, the noblest gift you gave
Came from you out beyond the grave:
The greatest was our Serra, he
Who lit your torch beside the sea.
Who made your dreams come true, who laid
The first stones of our city, made
The sweet bells of Dolores ring,
Whose echoes in our spirits sing.

Saint Francis, sometimes in the mist
You and Fra Serra keep a tryst.
Each sandaled and in robe of brown,
Under Tamalpais looking down—
You from far Umbria's wooded slopes,
Where first you built heroic hopes—
Serra from Carmel's piny hill,
Where long he worked Love's mighty will.
Attended by a dream you went,
Made comrade love a sacrament.
You laid on Serra your soul's great theme:
You passed to him your gift of dream.

And do you sometimes looking back
Ponder on what the world would lack
If you two gentlemen of God
Had not here planted rood and rod?
For it was from your souls of might
The City took its early sight.
And still the spirit of your dreams
Whispers in all her nobler themes.
Wherever Mercy stops the tears
We get vibration from your years.
Wherever Peace repels the sword
We touch the Christ that you adored.
Wherever Justice guards the poor

45

We hear your words that still endure.
Wherever men in this cold air
Turn to be Brothers, you are there!

Great priest and hero! See, we come,
To tell your toil and martyrdom.
We come, in these less earnest years,
To utter praise and reverent cheers—
To speak some words: of honoring
To you, our lowly barefoot king—
King over self, king over greed,
King whose one cry was human need.
Now as your spirit above us bends,
Stretching your hands to bless, oh give
Us the great knowledge how to live—
How to be comrades, noble friends.

Assisi

Alfred Noyes

I know a city on a hill, a mountain's castled crown,
Where, like the stairs the angels tread, the streets go
    up and down,
A city very small and kind and full of strange re-
    nown.

It stands upon an eastern height and looks towards
    the West.
Far off, it sees Perugia, its ancient foe, at rest;
And all the birds of Italy are gathered to its breast.

So small, so kind, but smaller far in the dim gulf
    below,
The world of men and all the tides that toss them
    to and fro,
While on its crag that city stands, crowned with the
    sunset glow.

Still, like a lean dark cypress there, against the clouds
    on high,
Brother of sun and moon and star, he towers into
    the sky,
As long ago, with arms up-stretched, while all things
    else went by.

Stone of his own immortal hill has made those ram-
parts bright,
The warm white stone that glows at dusk with a
soft unearthly light,
And delicate tones of heaven's own rose while the
plains are lost in night.

They told me of the lamp-lit tomb where dust in
dust was laid,
Of painted wings from Paradise that on their walls
decayed;
But not of this, this flower of light, that fades, and
cannot fade.

They did not tell me how it chanced that the small
bright streets were bare,
And hushed for love, as love went up, by cloister and
winding stair,
Till a little lamp-lit window shone like an altar lit
for prayer.

Oh bravely, bravely flash the swords beneath St.
Peter's dome.
Proudly the silver trumpets ring across the world
from Rome;
But this was on a higher hill, and a little nearer
home.

A little nearer home that night, when skies had
    ceased to glow;
And the great plain of Umbria was dark as death
    below,
Assisi grew into the light, as flowers and children
    grow.

The Nestling Church at Ovingdean

Alfred Noyes

The nestling church at Ovingdean
    Was fragrant as a hive in May;
And there was nobody within
    To preach, or praise, or pray.

The sunlight slanted through the door,
    And through the panes of painted glass
When I stole in, alone, once more
    To feel the ages pass.

Then, through the dim gray hush there droned
    An echoing plain-song on the air,
As if some ghostly priest intoned
    An old Gregorian there.

Saint Chrysostom could never lend
    More honey to the heavenly spring
Than seemed to murmur and ascend
    On that invisible wing.

So small he was, I scarce could see
　　My girdled brown hierophant;
But only a Franciscan bee
　　In such a bass could chant.

His golden Latin rolled and boomed.
　　It swayed the altar-flowers anew,
Till all that hive of worship bloomed
　　With dreams of sun and dew.

Ah, sweet Franciscan of the May,
　　Dear chaplain of the fairy queen,
You sent a singing heart away
　　That day, from Ovingdean.

A Sermon of Saint Francis

Edward F. Garesché, S.J.

'Twas at Assisi, of a summer's eve,
And gentle Francis stood and blessed the throng
Of plodding townsmen weary fain for home.
Then raised his voice, and spake his yearning heart:
"Brothers, I love ye all, I bid ye home
To sweetest rest, now the hard day is done.
For Jesus loved you, simple men of toil,
Yea, toiled like you, and weary was for home.
And when I see you pass, meseems I see
My tired Lord walk 'mid your brotherhood.
He IS among you. Brothers, ye must walk
Most reverent now, for He is at your side.
Are ye not Christian men? Have ye not spent
Your strength and sweat and labor for His love?
And will He fail to bear you company?
'If any labor, heavily burdened'—list
His loving tones—'let him but come to Me;
I will refresh him, I will be his rest.'
So thou, poor man, that feeble art and old,
Lean on His arm. And thou, my gentle boy,
Too tender still for toil, if thou hast woe
In thy young heart, quick tell it to thy Lord.

And you, poor mothers, homeward to the nest
Where your dear fledglings wait, and group them
    round,
And tell them all, that He Who taketh thought
For the young ravens when they cry for food
Hath endless care of them, providing love."

Saint Francis Endeth His Sermon

Louise Imogen Guiney

"And now, my clerks who go in fur or feather
Or brighter scale, I bless you all. Be true
To your true Lover and Avenger, whether
By land or sea ye die the death undue.
Then proffer man your pardon; and together
Track him to Heaven, and see his heart made new.

"From long ago one hope hath in me thriven,
Your hope, mysterious as the scented May:
Not to Himself your titles God hath given
In vain, nor only for our mortal day.
O doves! how from The Dove shall ye be driven?
O darling lambs! ye with The Lamb shall play."

53

Saint Francis and the Birds

Robert Hugh Benson

Once Saint Francis of Assisi saw a crowd of little
    birds
So he preached a sermon to them, and they listened
    to his words:
"Praise the Lord, my little Sisters, for the Lord, your
    God, is good;
In the ark that Noah made He saved your fathers
    from the flood."

Pleased because he called them "Sisters," all the
    birds spread out their wings
And flew down to Brother Francis, who could say
    such pretty things.
"Praise the Lord, my little Sisters, for the Lord, your
    God, is good,
And He gives you trees for houses, streams for drink
    and grain for food."

Then they stretched their necks and bowed their
    heads until they touched the sod,
While he told them they must study always to give
    praise to God.

Lastly with the Cross he blessed them, and their
   faith the birds confessed,
Flying off in four battalions, North and South and
   East and West.

Out of all the lovely deeds that Francis did at sweet
   Assisi,
I have chosen only this, because its lesson is so
   easy:
"Praise the Lord, and love His creatures, bird and
   beast, as well as men."
Sweet Saint Francis of Assisi, would that he were here
   again!

A Thought About Saint Francis

Denis A. McCarthy

Sometimes when I am walking in a wood
    Where there are birds, I wish Saint Francis, he
From his high station in the Place of Good
    Might suddenly appear and walk with me.
For then I know, in answer to his smile,
    The robin and the wren and every other
Would cease their merry singing for a while
    And come and listen to their Elder Brother.

I think it would be wonderful to see
    The lark drop down without the least alarm,
And the shy blue-bird leave the maple tree
    To perch upon the saint's outstretchèd arm;
To mark how even the sparrow for a space
    Would keep the pleasant woodland peace unbroken
To gaze upon the dear Saint Francis' face
    And hear the words of heavenly kindness spoken.

To me the birds will never fly although
    I love them well and fain would have them come.
They seem to fear from my rude hand a blow
    Instead of what it holds for them, a crumb.

And so when I am walking in a wood
  Where there are birds, I wish Saint Francis, he
Were at my side that, seeing him so good,
  They then might also venture close to me.

The Roses of Saint Francis

Thomas S. Jones, Jr.

The brother of the wind and sun bare-shod
  Came singing to the cave where long ago
  Two saints beheld the peaks of heaven glow
And sought the way with precept, rule and rod;
Shy creatures watched, as from the nettled sod
  Beneath his hands grew flowers of burning snow,
  And learned the starry law the angels know
That love alone can reach the heights of God.

His song of praise forever seems to ring
  When birds are waking or when shepherds rest
    Beside their lambs within a cavern's gloom;
And ever at the coming of the Spring,
  In the wild garden his pierced feet once pressed
    Where briars flourished only roses bloom.

From Poverello

Benjamin F. Musser

There is a sorrow in the hills tonight,
A plaintive restlessness among the leaves
That sadly turn from mellow afterlight
Colored across the evening and eaves
Of houses; there is murmuring unrest
In starling song, and in each woven nest
Disturbance broods; the hills, articulate
With pent-up words, mutter against their fate
And rumble down the valleys in their stern
Male grief, and seem to bend in grieving weight:
The world is hungering for his return.

If brother wolf and fishes feel the blight
Of his long absence; if the swallow grieves
And turtle-doves pause, worried, from their flight
To rest again upon his ashen sleeves;
If the lamb seeks that fire-concealing breast
And even brother fly would join the quest
For him whose love would not discriminate
Between the creatures; if there radiate,
At thought of him, intenser beams that yearn
From brother sun, all nature tries to state
The world is hungering for his return.

Discalced Prince, with love illuminate
Till you of all men best could penetrate
To Love Divine, with heart a flooded urn,
Speak to *His Heart* of orphan hearts that wait:
The world is hungering for *His* return.

Bell-Birds

Benjamin F. Musser

Dark as a bell that, from the mist-hung tower,
    Breaks into luminous song,
So does your heart, in its light-shedding power,
    Flood me the whole day long.

For in my cavern, not untenanted,
    Your chiming heart now swings;
The bats of fear have fluttered up and fled,
    And every bell-bird sings.

And every bell-bird, wheeling out and in
    My tower, to dusk from dawn
Blesses you with his clatter-clapper din
    Around that carillon.

Presumption

Eileen Duggan

The searchers of majesty shall all be slain by glory
And who am I to murmur against that prophecy,
Who will be fortunate to reach its marches,
Its last court's windiest arches?
And yet my poor Malvolian mind
Dreams saints its kind
And with an insolence
Beyond defense
Chooses its company
Among their chivalry.
Not Joan, that living banner
Of destined, fiery manner,
Nor John of Calvary
Hedged in by ecstasy.
Teresa of the glancing wit
Was never of a cloudy fit
And dreamers wince away from common sense,
But Bernadette would do. Men called her dense.
I like the ones that were not always just,
Whose palm was won in whorls of dust—
Peter the first and best of all
Because of the cock's call,

And Magdalen, her body's blame
Burnt in a crucible of shame,
Augustine, once his mother's cark
With lusts like lions in the dark,
And the great flying soul of Paul
Who once was Saul.
Then the superb de Sales, a holy crane,
As easy-minded as a plain,
Or small Assisi, God's gay bat,
With love as lofty as a ghat
And in his live improvidence
A dare to stock-still sense.
And I who in the flesh would fall,
Am homely with them all:
So can a linen samite seem
In the republic of a dream.

Saint Francis of Assisi

Shane Leslie

Francis, thou wast lonely plying
For thy bread from door to door,
Till God heard thy bitter sighing
For His Wounds and for His poor.

Till He bade thee all things leaving
Love the Lady Poverty,
Whom in joyfulness receiving
Thou didst wed as poor as thee.

Blind to earthen pomp and glory
Thou didst see the Crucified,
When the Scars, God won in story,
Smote thee, hands and feet and side.

And His Eyes upon the mountain
Left each burning Wound with thee,
As they looked upon the fountain
Of thy soul in ecstasy.

Now thy feet like ensigns glowing
March above the starry plain,
And thy hands are rich bestowing
Love for all thy children's pain.

To the Father glory giving
And the wondrous-wounded Son,
Let us glorify the Living
Spirit ever Three in One.

A Broad Minded Bishop Rebukes
the Verminous Saint Francis

Gilbert K. Chesterton

If Brother Francis pardoned Brother Flea,
There still seems need of such strange charity
Seeing he is, for all his gay goodwill,
Bitten by funny little creatures still.

Come Up to Umbria

Charles Phillips

Time passes, and the years;
But one, new come
Upon the ancient warning, sudden hears
Over life's clamor and discordant hum
A singing voice
Calling and summoning with a song that makes his
  heart rejoice:

Come up, come up with me to Umbria!
Come, climb the high ascents and hilltop ways
Of old Assisi, where once Francis trod
Singing his soul to God.

There is an air
Of deathless beauty there,
Of ageless life, that breathes, that moves, that speaks,
Below, above,
Through endless songful days,
Through golden moons of fructifying fire,
Through starbreak and the blue ethereal wonder
Of silver-veiléd nights,
Whose lucent dreams
Of youth, of love, of all the soul delights,
Awake and stir

In wide-eyed azure skies,
Or in dim shadows and the moonlit blur
Of cypressed slopes and olive groves, or under
The rush of gloom-splashed mountain streams
Snow-fed from spotless peaks
Of virgin light.

Come up, come up with me to Umbria!
Where, dawn or dusk, and all the smiling day,
The beauty-presséd soul laughs out or cries,
Pierced by God's bright stigmata of desire,
With song that is a prayer,
With prayer that is a song of joyous praise.

Come up, come up to Umbria with me,
Where still—as when the thorny, flowerlike way
Of blessed Francis lay
Along these steep-flung paths—the days declare,
And the unfolding nights
Proclaim an echo, and the skyey heights
Announce and publish clarionlike and clear,
Shouting it mightily,
Below, above:
"There is a deathless beauty here,
There is a fadeless youth,
Ageless as love
And endless as the truth!"

Cloister

Charles L. O'Donnell, C.S.C.

"Show me your cloister," asks the Lady Poverty of the friars. And they, leading her to the summit of a hill, showed her the wide world, saying: "This is our cloister: O Lady Poverty!"

Well, that were a cloister: for its bars
Long strips of sunset, and its roof the stars.

Four walls of sky, with corridors of air
Leading to chapel, and God everywhere.

Earth beauteous and bare to lie upon,
Lit by the little candle of the sun.

The wind gone daily sweeping like a broom—
For these vast hearts it was a narrow room.

The Wolf of Gubbio to Saint Francis

Anna McClure Sholl

Dear holy Saint, you have given me loving counsel,
And I reverence you for it.
But before I promise anything,
Just one word about those people up at Gubbio—
They're worse than the animals
Because they know better!—
They lie and steal and cheat each other,
And beat their poor overworked horses
Until they drop in their tracks—
They call themselves Christians!
Isn't it enough to make even a wolf laugh!
Please tell them for me
That if everybody loved us as you love us
There would soon be no wild animals
Nor beasts of prey.
—Yes, certainly, I'll reform, I'll be a good wolf.
But, mind you, Saint Francis,
I am doing this entirely for you,
Not for those people up at Gubbio!

The Little Black Hen

Armel O'Connor

We heard the little hen was black,
And nothing hen-wise did she lack—
Besides her pow'r of laying eggs,
This hen had feathers down her legs.

Just like a tame dove's were her feet
('Twas unexpected this, but sweet),
And oh! her chicks so many were,
She couldn't keep them under her.

One of the very best of men
Once dreamed about this little hen:
And when the sleeping Saint awoke,
He pondered long before he spoke.

"I am that hen, in stature small,
So black by nature that I crawl
Instead of, like the simple dove,
Seeking the sky with wings of love.

"I am not able to defend
My chicks and those the Lord will send.
Take, Holy Church, my offerings
Beneath the shadow of thy wings."

When later on, he saw the Pope,
He told him of his ardent hope. . . .
Honorius blessed the little hen
Who wasn't black—whose chicks were men.

Appreciation à la Mode

Armel O'Connor

A Lady in the latest gown
Speaks to me thus in London Town:
"Of all the Saints that really were,
I almost think that I prefer
Francesco of Assisi. He
Seems absolutely *sweet* to me."
Then to her looking-glass she goes
And puts fresh powder on her nose.

Many a mile from London Town
A happy spirit, clad in brown,
Ragged but woodland-scented, clean,
Dances and sings before his Queen.
Phantom but ringing laughter fills
Wide heavens over noble hills,
When Fashion deigns to call him *sweet*,
Who bled from heart and hands and feet.

Saint Francis

Eliot Kays Stone

Saint Francis called to the birds,
   And they came from field and wood,
And they harkened to his words,

For the words he spoke were good.
   And all the feathered folk
Fluttered about his hood.

A great horned owl awoke,
   And drifted down from a tree,
And blinked as St. Francis spoke:

". . . . The God of the land and sea,
   The God of the earth and sky,
Is the God of you . . . and me.

We cannot answer, 'Why.'
   There is no answer thereof;
We can only live and die.

But our God is a God of Love,
   And we are all in his care,
The peregrine and the dove.

Little Brothers of the Air,
   No sparrow falls to the ground,
   No feather swirls around,
But the heart of our God is there."

From *To a Thrush*

Thomas A. Daly

Sing clear, O! throstle,
Thou golden-tongued apostle
And little brown-frocked brother
Of the loved Assisian!
Sing courage to the mother,
Sing strength into the man,
For they, who in another May
Trod Hope's scant wine from grapes of pain,
Have tasted in thy song today
The bitter-sweet red lees again.
To them in whose sad May-time thou
Sang'st comfort from thy maple bough,
To tinge the presaged dole with sweet,
O! prophet then, be prophet now
And paraclete!

That fateful May! The pregnant vernal night
Was throbbing with the first faint pangs of day,
The while with ordered urge toward life and light,
Earth-atoms countless groped their destined way;
And one full-winged to fret
Its tender oubliette,

The warding mother-heart above it woke,
   Darkling she lay in doubt, then, sudden wise,
Whispered her husband's drowsy ear and broke
   The estranging seal of slumber from his eyes:
   "My hour is nigh: arise!"

Already, when, with arms for comfort linked,
   The lovers at an eastward window stood,
The rosy day, in cloudy swaddlings, blinked
   Through misty green new-fledged in Wister Wood.
         Breathless upon this birth
         The still-entrancèd earth
Seemed brooding, motionless in windless space.
   Then rose thy priestly chant, O! holy bird!
And heaven and earth were quickened with its grace;
   To tears two wedded souls were moved who heard,
   And one, unborn, was stirred!

O! Comforter, enough that from thy green
   Hid tabernacle in the wood's recess
To those care-haunted lovers thou, unseen,
   Should'st send thy flame-tipped song to cheer and
      bless.
         Enough for them to hear
         And feel thy presence near;
And yet when he, regardful of her ease,

Had led her back by brightening hall and stair
To her own chamber's quietude and peace,
   One maple-bowered window shook with rare,
   Sweet song—and thou wert there!

Hunter of souls! the loving chase so nigh
   Those spirits twain had never come before.
They saw the sacred flame within thine eye;
   To them the maple's depths quick glory wore,
      As though God's hand had lit
      His altar-fire in it,
And made a fane, of virgin verdure pleached,
   Wherefrom thou might'st in numbers musical
Expound the age-sweet words thy Francis preached
   To thee and thine, of God's benignant thrall
   That broodeth over all.
And they, athirst for comfort, sipped thy song,
   But drank not yet thy deeper homily.
Not yet, but when parturient pangs grew strong,
   And from its cell the young soul struggled free—
      A new joy, trailing grief,
      A little crumpled leaf,
Blighted before it burgeoned from the stem—
   Thou, as the fabled robin to the rood,
Wert minister of charity to them;
   And from the shadows of sad parenthood
   They heard and understood.

74

Makes God one soul a lure for snaring three?

   Ah! surely; so this nursling of the nest,

This teen-touched joy, ere birth anoint of thee,

   Yet bears thy chrismal music in her breast.

      Five Mays have come and sped

      Above her sunny head,

And still the happy song abides in her.

   For though on maimed limbs the body creeps,

It doth a spirit house whose pinions stir

   Familiarly the far cerulean steeps

   Where God His mansion keeps.

      So come, O! throstle

      Thou golden-tongued apostle

And little brown-frocked brother

   Of the loved Assisian!

Sing courage to the mother,

   Sing strength into the man,

That she who in another May

   Came out of heaven, trailing care,

May never know that sometimes gray

   Earth's roof is and its cupboard bare,

To them in whose sad May-time thou

Sang'st comfort from thy maple bough,

   To tinge the presaged dole with sweet,

O! prophet then, be prophet now

   And paraclete!

San Francesco d'Assisi

Catherine Parmenter

I will move quietly within this place,
Where God reveals His soul so wondrously,
In bird and flower and brook and wind and tree,
In sun and sky, the glory of His face.
I will go silently, alone; and still
Not quite alone, for what is that—a mist?
Perhaps—but here, I think, he keeps the tryst:
A little gray-robed figure on the hill.
I know the healing hands, the brave, clear eyes;
I hear the gentle voice. O robins, sing!
And to his heart beloved memories bring
Of happy days beneath Italian skies.
Dear God what miracle is this? I see
Leaves, softly silver, from an olive tree!

Saint Francis Weds the Three Maidens
(After Sassetta)

Helene Mullins

O Birds and stones, rejoice and pray,
O fishes crowd to the edge of the sea;
Your little brother weds today
Obedience, Poverty, Chastity.

Poverty to keep the lamp-wicks trim
And bake the daily bread,
Obedience to walk with him,
And Chastity to share his bed.

O stones, come clattering; birds, come singing,
Fishes, come dancing on the tides;
Never did wedding-bells go ringing
For three such comely brides:

Two to curb his frivolity,
One to make him quiet and wise,
And all to be with him loyally
Till death close down his eyes.

Saint Francis

Dorothy Bennett

Francis spoke to the birds
   By the blue Italian sea,
Feeding them full with his words—
   "Oh, little brothers," said he,
"I bring you the love of God
   And the hope of eternity.
The thousand years since He trod
   Up steep Gethsemane
Is but the dust of the street,"
   Said Francis, "to His feet!"

Francis spoke to the beast,
   To Messer Death spoke he,
"Our brother the wolf, not least
   Are you in God's beauty!
Your strength is as a hill,
   It is a dark pine tree."
And Messer Death was still,
   His head on Francis' knee.
And in his eyes the red
   And awful glare was dead.

Four hundred years is a breath,
  A thousand years is a day,
Still men fear Messer Death
  Since Francis went that way.
Yet still the sparrows keep
  Their tryst with verities.
The years are but a sweep
  Of street-dust in their eyes!
Give us, then, world without end
  And Messer Death, our friend!

The Lady Poverty

Evelyn Underhill

I met her on the Umbrian hills:
  Her hair unbound, her feet unshod;
As one whom secret glory fills
  She walked, alone with God.

I met her in the city street:
  Oh, changed was all her aspect then!
With heavy eyes and weary feet
  She walked, alone with men.

From Saint Francis of Assisi

"Who went to meet death singing"
—THOMAS OF CELANO

Jane C. Crowell

He went to meet death singing—
That saint of bygone years,
Who held the purest laughter
As much divine as tears.

He went to meet death singing—
And all the way he trod
Proved courtesy unchanging
A quality of God.

He went to meet death singing—
His life of joy outrun
Whom Dante for his fervor
Did liken to the sun.

He went to meet death singing—
And to the blessed throng
He soared with Christ triumphant,
Himself a soul of song. . . .

The Blessing of Saint Francis

Sister Maura

"The Lord bless thee and keep thee; the Lord show
His face to thee and have mercy on thee; the Lord
turn His countenance to thee and give thee peace."

Seven times the centiple wheels of life have whirled
Since Francis, in his brave abandonment,
Committed his young way to a free world
And the great hand of God; above him bent
The pitying sky; he saw in the sun and moon
And the light of stars, the smile of God, and heard
His voice in the music of the sea, the croon
Of the wilful wind, and the joyous lilt of a bird:
He loved in every soul drawing human breath
The spirit of the Maker, whose best peace
Followed his shining steps to the bourne of death
And filled the orbit of his life's increase.
Trust, mercy, peace—all those who love him will
Know in their lives his triple blessing still.

From The Minstrel of God

Clement Wood

O sweet strange minstrel of the joyous singing,
When the torn lands lay bleeding in the dark
With dripping sword and ripping lancehead bringing
Death to harsher life, like Sister Lark
You trilled your melodies at the ear of heaven,
A halo of harmony above the pain,
Until the world, from which your soul was driven,
Woke to a little loveliness again.
Minstrel of God, you knew that they spoke ill
Who called the One you loved a Man of Sorrow:
Others had made His golden singing still;
And you could see a lightening tomorrow
When song and the sweet salvation of mirth
Should rule again over the reddened earth.

The noisy swallows quieted at your teaching;
The shrill grasshopper gave you heart to sing;
The falcon was your angelus; your preaching
Went most to souls that heard you on the wing.
Even the wolf, his steel jaws hot from plunder,
Tamed at your soft whispering, as he
Brought his harsh and hungry nature under

Your love sway. Brother Wind and Sister Sea,
Moon and Brother Sun, with these you spoke,
Granting kind greeting to the Brother Fire
Who healed your body. To this varied folk
You had a word to lift their longing higher.
    Only one beast hid snarling in his den:
    You could not tame the wild lost tribe called men.

Franciscan

Katherine Brégy

I reach out arms of love to you,
    shadowy, immemorial mountains,
And to you, transient clouds drawing
    white dreams across the sky—
And to you, tiny golden chipmunk
Peering up from the pine-brush
    suddenly with questioning eye!

Alien

Mary Brent Whiteside

He crouches in the chapel, on his knees,
   With matted hair that hangs in dusky strands;
   Apart and strange, among the little bands
Of worshipers, for he is not as these.
Alone! and yet a deeper vision sees
   That near this alien with his grimy hands,
   The Little Poor Man of Assisi stands,
As Giotto painted him upon a frieze.

I knew one luminous Italian spring!
   "Your province? Is it Umbria?" I ask.
   The weariness falls from him like a mask,
And all his visage is a shining thing,
   As though some deathless master of his race
   Inscribed a sudden message on his face.

Saint Francis of Assisi

Tom Sweeney

While hastening through his pilgrimage on earth,
The traveler, Saint Francis, learned the truth:
No thing that God creates can be uncouth;
The world is filled with beauty wed to mirth;
All living creatures prove a Father's hand;
The rocks, if mute, deserve our reverence;
The love of God can brook no severance
Between the vassals tenanting His land.

He catechized the birds; addressed the fire.
He would not fell a tree or cut a flower—
For God made all and why should man destroy!
The moon's our sister, clad in proud attire!
Disclaiming wealth, ambition, earthly power,
Like Christ, he left a note of mounting joy.

Music

Daniel Sargent

Saint Francis prayed in a double darkness chill,
In the dark of his heart, in the dark that came on the
hill,
And his cell was dark, but his heart was darker still.

Saint Francis prayed: if only he once might hear
One strain of the music bright that is Heaven's cheer,
One single strain, hear now on this dark earth here.

And an angel shone in the night of his double black,
In the little cell that cabined his utter lack,
Like a lightning flash, but hushed without thunder-
crack.
And the angel poised a bow, and he pressed a bright
Viola to his heart like his heart's delight,
And the angel flamed like the very heart of the night.

And the angel moved the bow, and there leaped a
strain,
Clear as a song which long in heaven has lain.
It cleft the dark as a rainbow cleaves the rain.

It cleft the heart of the saint, it cleft through stone,
It cleft to the hush where man and his God are lone,
And the saint lay cloven in twain, till noonday shone.

86

Prayer for the Hunted

Daniel Henderson

When shall the panting fox
  Discover its shield
In the bosom of man
  From the baying field?

When shall the fowler turn
  And rend his snare
As the meshed oriole
  Utters its prayer?

Francis, gospeler
  To the listening wood;
Cuthbert, whom petrels heard
  And understood,

Cannot mercy live
  In the hearts of men?
Speak through us with love
  To the wild again!

In Memoriam

Dorothy Frances Gurney

Oh! my Saint Francis of the gentle eyes,
Who made for God so high a song of praise,
And loved so deeply that of His which strays
That thou dost wear His Wounding for a prize;
Say, didst thou take his hand in Paradise
And lead him gladly up its golden ways
To crown him for God's poet with the bays
And teach him still profounder mysteries?

Or didst thou only lay the hands that healed
Upon his head to still the tired brain,
And even as a mother soothes to rest
The child she washes from its truant stain
Didst thou so bear him, naked, clean, annealed,
And lay him like a babe on Jesu's breast?

Saint Francis of Assisi Talks With a Priest

Jay G. Sigmund

My son, this is the very world I knew;
Oh, think you not it suffers much of change!
A man-ruled world this is; then why should you
Or I or anybody deem it strange?

Here are the lepers and the rich and poor;
Here there is good and sin and worldly greed;
Centuries come and vanish to be sure
But the same need is here, the same need.

Need of an understanding of that One—
That Great Poet-Healer and His teachings:
Need of appreciation of God's Son—
Less of the platitudes contained in preachings.

Simple, you say? Yes, simple, I admit,
But the world was always chary as a whole
Of one who kissed a leper, who would sit
At the board of Christ to feed his starving soul.

This is the same world, my son, the same;
These are the same men who hewed the tree;
Here is the same Pilate with a new name—
But the same Christ is here Who guided me.

From The Death of an Italian Beggar

Brother Clement, O.F.M.

Larks and the angels make a stir,
And the sky calls,
And a great song tenderer
Than light, falls.

Larks, soft singing, come and go;
And the light,
And the great winds of heaven blow
From cloudless gold to night.

His memory goes from song to older song,
And the larks sing.
The hour draws back, and long and long
Is remembering.

*   *   *

Now the birds are quiet and the wood
Is quiet, and the hearts of outcast men
Fill with the old solitude
Again.

After the last lark passed, a star
Passed, carried radiantly
As on a cloud, or on a sea
That carries radiance far.

Now the song comes softer, and is done.
Softer than song the bird flies.
Now he has passed, but the sun
Passes not, not from the eyes!

The Rich Man of Assisi

Sister M. Benvenuta

Pietro Bernardone's son
   Was richer than a king. They say
   He found a field where treasures lay,
And bartered all to buy it. None
   In all the land so rich as he
   To wed the Lady Poverty.

Though princes of the earth should cry
   Him welcome, lofty palace roof
   Seemed low to him, who held aloof,
Nor set his lower than the sky;
   While all his wealthy kith and kin
   Brought gems and furs to robe him in.

With ermine hangings for his bed
   Came Sister Snow in winter time;
   And Sister Rain and Brother Rime
With pearls and diamonds crowned his head
   Till Brother Sun, in kingly play,
   Would come and fling them all away.

And yet this Dives, lusting still,
  Would rifle with his miser's art
  The very coffers of God's Heart,
Till on a day he had his will:
  From Heaven's height a seraph came,
  And brought him rubies red as flame.

Green-arrassed halls with perfume strewn
  House him, of all men wealthiest,
  With ruby buckle at his breast,
And ruby-studded glove and shoon.
  O rich man Francis, look on me,
  So poor, who crave an alms of thee.

The Birds and Francis

Louis Untermeyer

The path ran out. The clouds, no longer fleecy,
Ravelled their wool in solid twist on twist.
The mountains swam away from him. Assisi
Crumbled its stone in alchemy of mist.
His mind was elsewhere, groping to determine
What shape to give his sermon.

Now all was lost. The road, the scene, himself.
The snow had wolfed down Gubbio. Nothing stirred
Except one thrush too cold to preen himself,
But not too cold to prove himself a bird;
Gripping his glassy perch, intent on trying
To prove it without flying.

"What thing," he twittered, "cares to come and freeze
    here
Where none but the pale Trapper stalks the wood?
Only a bird could be so much at ease here;
Yet this is never an owl for all his hood,
But a dark creature, motherless and whelpless.
I'll call help for the helpless."

Suddenly the smooth air was torn with vying
Fragments of voices curious and shrill.
Whereat the saint, now conscious of the crying,
Waited until his audience grew still,
And, half by habit, half preoccupation
Addressed his congregation.

"Children," he said, "we live with mysteries
So intimate that we are seldom awed.
Our brother is stout noon, our sister is
Soft night with largesse from the lap of God.
All are within that sacred family."
Thus he began his homily.

"Space that appears a void and infinite canyon
Steadies and props this lurching world; the air,
Kinder than earth, is our unvexed companion,
Whose strong, sustaining arms are everywhere.
No bird can fall, however man may stumble,
While the true heart is humble.

"Humble and not too happy; self-denying;
Choosing a little lower than the least;
So let us live and save ourselves from flying
Where pride betrays what only pride increased.
In love with poverty, ambition loathing,
Bow and desire nothing."

The saint paused for the final benediction,
Waiting a moment for his flock to rise;
He did not see with what quick circumspection
Those troubled eyes appealed to other eyes.
And then the birds, with rapid, sidelong glances,
Began their sermon to Saint Francis.

"Father," they sang, "we have been ever burdened
By man's fear and the limit of his thought.
In the beginning was the finite word-end—
And in the little ends has he been caught.
We have no words, no snaring thought; we seize on
Reasons beyond your reason.

"Nothing we know was fashioned to arrest us,
Nor was rich earth created for denial;
Height was made high and hazardous to test us,
And the proud heart to trust the ultimate trial.
No less than All flows from the open heaven.
Ask—and it shall be given."

They waited. Then they shed upon that swart head,
A lingering benediction without words.
Only the thrush was left and he departed,
Still twittering, to join the other birds
Whose happy syllables were heard a mile hence. . . .
And Francis bowed in silence.

Spendthrift

Sister M. Genoveva, C.S.C.

A spendthrift youth, Assisi's gayest lad
In joyous giving spent his father's gold,
The princely Francis in rich velvet clad,
A merchant's son, with soul of kingly mold.
"A fool," said Bernardone, "he has no care
For gain, and even of his spirit's bliss
He cannot keep the whole, but needs must share,
And press it on a leper with a kiss."

His father's store-house barred, he pilfered love,
And filled his heart from heaven's treasury;
Then since he heard no censure from above,
He gave to all earth's children lavishly;
Nor thieves, nor woodland creatures thought too low;
He shared it with the Wolf of Gubbio.

Saint Francis

Amanda Benjamin Hall

I think it was in such a greenery
As this, he bade the birds be orthodox;
Parishioners who came in eager flocks,
Who listened with bright-eyed credulity
To Holy Gospel. Hushed their happy din,
Those feathered converts knew a sweet despair,
Repented greatly of each trifling sin,
And little peccadillo of the air.

So innocence from godliness was fed.
And who, in this far day, shall disavow
Each wore a tiny halo round its head,
As piously they perched along the bough?
I hear them as the good saint heard them then,
With flutelike voices crying out, "Amen!"

Saint Francis

Horace Shipp

We thought that we had tricked you, Poverello,
Walled you in marble, coffined you in gold;
But you laugh last, the same quaint simple fellow,
God's little sparrow, lively as of old.

We thought we had burked your question, but you
    pose it
Pertinent as ever and unanswered still;
And we must choose a way because you chose it:
The outspread kingdoms, or the lonely hill;

Plaudits of men or pains of Christ's own choosing,
Pierced side and serving hands and feet that trod
His path of love and loneliness; and losing
The world for this you gained the peace of God.

This was your wisdom in its last unfolding;
This your divine dilemma; and we know
We, too, must choose: the path of pride and holding,
Or your way, Saint, of love and letting go.

Saint Francis

Brother Rudolph, C.F.X.

Thin ghost of a man
In rough habit of brown,
How he stumbled and ran
Through the streets of the town:
To the woods and the stream
Where the soft night winds blow,
Where a troubadour's dream
Could blossom and grow.

Men said he was mad,
Had been cursed from his birth,
But the whole world was sad
So he drenched it with mirth.
And the birds wheeling by
Loved a monk who romanced,
So they dropped from the sky
When he capered and danced.

His heart was on fire
With a wild burning love,
With a flaming desire
For the God up above.

And the paeans he sang
Held such rapture and glee
That the universe rang
With his minstrelsy!

Oh, Francis, return,
For the world has grown gray:
It will grieve and will yearn
For the Christlike and gay
Till the music you made
And the lilt of your song—
God's own serenade—
Rings out clear and strong!

From Saint Francis' Lesson to His Brothers

Sister of the Poor Clares

My Brothers, when the north wind bites us sharply
And would with our poor garments rudely toy,
Be not downcast, dear brothers, but rejoicing,
   For this is truly joy!

When Brother Sun upon our heads would tender
His kiss of peace with burning rays of heat,
And we have naught to serve us as a shelter,
   Ah, brothers, this is sweet!

When we are weak with hunger, and are thirsty,
And no one gives a crust, or drop to drink,
O brothers, let us then be glad and joyous,
   For this is bliss, I think! . . .

When we are mocked, insulted, struck and jeered at,
As through the town we meekly go our way,
O brothers mine, let us be gay and gladsome
   With brimming joy, I say! . . .

In other gifts of God we cannot glory
For they proceed not from ourselves; the loss
Of all things else we can accept, rejoicing,
 And glory in the Cross!

For when, for His dear sake, O little brothers,
We conquer self, and every fault destroy,
We give Christ all. Nailed up with Him we glory—
 And this is Perfect Joy!

Saint Francis to the Birds

Clement Cook, O.F.M.

Where parsley and lilies lie
Near a blue lake in spring,
He sat in a singing ring
Of small birds, finger-high.

"Before the bell we must part,
So feed on honeycomb
And find for your wings a home,
And find for your song a heart."

A Rhyme for Francis: October 4th

Eleanor Farjeon

The kinsmen of Francis
Were not as another's.
The birds were his sisters,
The beasts were his brothers.
These were his names
For the great and the small—
Was not God Father
Of him, and of all?

The night and the morning,
The water, the wind,
The star and the daisy,
Were each of his kind.
God was the Father
Of him and all others,
And flowers were his sisters,
And trees were his brothers.

"Brother, good morning!"
He said to Friar Sun.
"Sister, good even!"
To moon, the sweet Nun.
"God is our Father,
We know of no other,
And Death is my sister,
And Life is my brother."

"September 17"

(Feast of the Stigmata of St. Francis)

Sister M. Margaret Patricia

High Mass
Under the new
Bronze baldachino—
American industrial
Art—
(The Sequence is too long
Franciscan students
Monotone alternate verses.)

Adoration
Springs in the Preface of
Saint Francis
Stigmatized, the
Christ-man.

Remembering Assisium: boughs,
Huts and rocks; lepers and
Singing poverty, I thought of
Clare; recalled
The barrier of ashes
Francis strewed

Around himself when Clare besought
From him
One final sermon!

Today when solemn heaven
Rose and extolled
The Trinity, did not
The wounded one
Turn and across the
Circling concourse of
Franciscan ages
Bow to Clare?

And she
Her answering smile
In woman's wisdom hiding
Forever, as in Assisium's cloister
Her puzzlement; and, penance
Returning courtesy in
Merry tenderness,
Mark now around the
Glowing wounded feet
The ring of ashes?

Saint Francis' Wood

Alexander J. Cody, S.J.

A little chapel of pink tile,
A poplar grove, a broken stile:
We say with Peter, "Lord, 'tis good
To visit You in Francis' Wood."

The minnows in the placid brook
Forever read God's picture-book.

The pensive wolf sedately walks
Between the shadowed aisles and stalks.

The linnets in an aspen tree
Make matin's sweetest melody.

The sycamores in scarlet gowns
Are willingly God's forest clowns.

The eucalyptus' whispering breath
Tells secrets of sweet sister Death.

The scalloped-lichened mossy stone
Is Lady Poverty's own throne.

A stable's roof with winter stain
Recalls the spot where Christ had lain.

A little chapel of pink tile,
A poplar grove, a broken stile:
We say with Peter, "Lord, 'tis good
To visit You in Francis' Wood."

In My Garden

Alma L. Gray

When good St. Francis feeds his flock
   Beside my garden wall,
The marigold and four o'clock
   Stand tiptoe at his call.
The wren, the sparrow from the street,
   The vireos and jays,
Hold sweet communion at his feet
   And chant a song of praise.

When good St. Francis feeds his birds
   Above my flowering hedge,
The sunlight falls like sacred words
   Upon the marble ledge,
While from his niche the sculptured priest,
   With confidence unflawed,
Bids me, too, share the holy feast,
   The gardened Go-with-God.

The Wolf of Gubbio Speaks to Saint Francis

Sister Mary Monica, C.S.C.

I know thee well, brown friar,
The greenwood folk speak much
Of thee. In bush and briar
The feathered ones sing of the goodly word
Which thou dost bring to them of Christ the Lord.

Along the marshy edge
Of forest streams, the fish
Wait—staring through the sedge
Grass—hoping thou wilt pass their way once more
And speak to them—thou didst, they say—before.

The men of Gubbio
Good sires, do think thee mad,
'Tis said they deem thee so
For that thou holdest talk with beast and bird
And hearest wingèd sounds no man hath heard.

For that thou claimest kin
With fire and rain and moon,
Art frugal and deep in
The hills long watch dost keep alone. They swear
One saw thee pray with fire upon thy hair.

But I—I know not, friar,
If man or beast speak true.
I only know desire
To touch with my cool tongue the ruddy heat
Of those twin scarlet flames that pierce thy feet.

Lauds

Leonard Mahoney, S.J.

The robin is a mendicant,
A friar of the trees,
Who begs a breath of fragrant air
From cherry-scented breeze.

The robin is a troubadour,
Who sings to Sister Spring
The beauty of the budding rose
And of creation's King.

I Go to School

Sister M. Madeleva, C.S.C.

I seek a teacher and a rule,
Dear Brother Francis, and a school
Where I can learn to be a fool.

The world is erudite today;
The folk of Gubbio and thy gray
Brother Wolf are dead, they say.
   Sweet friend of Christ, thyself shalt be
   My book of gentle courtesy.

A single purse, a single cloak
Do scarce suffice for modern folk;
Such foolishness as once thou spoke
   About thy Lady Poverty,
   That, poverello, tell to me.

Bird songs in Umbria were sweet,
Or else, mayhap, thy quaint conceit
Found meanings now quite obsolete.
   God's little one, wilt share with me
   Thy sister birds' sweet psaltery?

Stars nebular and wise, indeed,
Above Averno shared thy creed
Of piercèd Heart and Wounds that bleed.
   Enamored Knight of Calvary,
    Teach me love's madmost ecstasy.

Behold my teacher and my rule;
Thyself, Saint Francis, art my school;
God give me grace to be a fool!

Things to Be Loved

Sister M. Madeleva, C.S.C.

The Carceri, soft rain in February,
These two stone oaks, this sky of Giotto's blue,
Beds of hepatica and fritillary
In this square garden plot that Francis knew:

These things are to be loved. I know. I love them
In their still world, uplifted from the plain.
I choose for you the diffident dearest of them,
White fritillaries in the Umbrian rain.

Roses for My King
(The Stigmata of Saint Francis)

Sister M. Madeleva, C.S.C.

If that my King should say,
"Fetch me of roses five most fair today,"
Where, think you, could I find
Flowers to please His heart, to please His mind?

Straight would I go to him,
Who stands forever next the seraphim,

And say, "Here, at his feet,
Are roses, Master, that Thy heart deems sweet.

"And from his hands there spring
Blossoms that worthy are of Thee, my King.

"One flower more doth bide
Within the lovely garden of his side.

"See how its petals part,—
O God, it is the blossom of his heart!"

Dear Master, bid me, pray,
Bring Thee of flowers the five most fair today;
Look Thou, where I will find
Roses to please Thy heart, to please Thy mind.

After the Thought of Saint Francis

Sister M. Maura, S.S.N.D.

Brother Ass, fretful, slothful,
dragging still the halter,
lifts the Lord Christ on his back
returning from the altar.
Monday, Tuesday, Wednesday,
Brother Ass goes to town;
Thursday, Friday, too, he goes,
not a mantle is laid down.
When you meet the homely beast
trudging down the street,
see beyond his tired eyes,
and beyond his thudding feet—
though no palm fronds mark his path,
no Hosannas break his way—
still the King goes with His beast,
watch for *Him* today.

Song of the Fire

Sister M. Maura, S.S.N.D.

Flame on the poppies and a gray mist weaves
shaken silver ashes on the young olive leaves;
St. Francis' joy is singing, singing on its lyre,
hymn to its Maker, song of the fire.

Sun on the petals and a petal is the sun,
lucent, tawny petal when Assisi's day is done;
Francis' heart goes singing, canticle or hymn,
hymn to the flame-gold along Assisi's rim.

White on the olive trees a full moon burns,
white through the narrow streets, white on the ferns;
Francis' lips are singing to an old French tune
song to the fire, fire on the moon.

But out beyond Assisi in the old Chapter House,
home alike of brethren and the gray field mouse,
though he cut the silken kindling, strand on strand,
pale, golden-yellow, brand on brand,

though his eyes gave benediction to the slender little
    pyre,

the slender, flaming brightness of the white-gold fire,
there was not a breath of singing, not a single burning
     word,
though the brethren listened silent, not a word was
     heard

for the birth of the golden flame, burning, flaming
     yet,
heaped with tender giving, heaped without regret,
the satin-silken kindling of the soft shining hair,
the wonder-woven kindling of the hair of Clare.

117

Marionette

Fray Angelico Chavez, O.F.M.

You should be the saint, St. Francis,
Of Marionettes, whose every move
In all their seeming mad-cap dances
Depends on strings pulled from above.

As in that scene of strange desires,
When God peered from the mountain's crest
And lifted you with golden wires
That pierced your hands and feet and breast.

I Vowed

Fray Angelico Chavez, O.F.M.

I vowed that I would not possess
Things having bulk of earthly dross,
Because my Lord in emptiness
Lay in the crib and on the cross.

The Lord was pleased, for He has blessed
My body's poorness and my soul's—
Behold, the treasures that He pressed
Into my hands are little holes.

Prayer to Saint Francis for Poverty

Liam Brophy

From cities' pyramids, untrammelled saint,
    Deliver us, from all this ponderous weight
Of merchandise that makes our spirits faint:
    Lay bare our lives, for it is growing late.

Strip us of these bright fabrics we have made
    Of woven Finance, break the narrow mould
Of our modernity: we are afraid
    To shake them from us lest our hearts grow cold.

From all that clogs and clutters life, and clings
    About our crouching, burdened hearts so we
Can never tell what way the song-thrush sings
    Come soon on naked feet and set us free.

Lo, we are hemmed and held a hundred ways—
    Impoverish us that our rich hearts may run
Like liberated larks to chant the praise
    Of bright and unobstructed Brother Sun.

Lift from us, in your gracious gentleness,
    This dead weight of our cold complexities
Lest wars' tornadoes strip us to excess
    And humble us to hell's simplicities.

Brother Dog

Luis Anibal Sanchez
From the Spanish by Muna Lee

In the enormous tragic silence of the night, Francis,
the monk of Assisi, with sunken eyes of immense
tenderness, caressed the white body, the snow-
white body, of a poor dog that died in the war.

To that body which had no soul, but which felt much,
loved much, suffered much, Francis has given a
tear and infinite pity.

Francis has wept, while afar nations made war.

It is the apocalyptic hour. Humanity is condensed into
one long shriek. Hate asserts its supremacy. The
great red cataclysm sows earth with tears and
blood; tears of the child and of the beloved,
and ancient crystallized tears of the venerable
mothers who weep in dark alcoves where the
cat whines sybaritically without knowing why.

Before the white body of the poor dog slain by chance
bullets, the divine Francis wept.

The Stone

Anne Morrow Lindbergh

There is a core of suffering that the mind
Can never penetrate or even find;
A stone that clogs the stream of my delight,
Hidden beneath the surface out of sight,
Below the flow of words it lies concealed.
It blocks my passage and it will not yield
To hammer blows of will, and still resists
The surgeon's scalpel of analysis.
Too hard for tears and too opaque for light,
Bright shafts of prayer splinter against its might.
Beauty cannot disguise nor music melt
A pain, undiagnosable but felt.

No sleep dissolves that stony stalagmite,
Mounting within the unconscious caves of night.

No solvent left but love. Whose love? My own?
And is one asked to love the harsh unknown?
I am no Francis who could kiss the lip
Of alien leper. Caught within the grip
Of world un-faith, I cannot even pray,
And must I love? Is there no other way?

Suffering without name or tongue or face,
Blindly I crush you in my dark embrace!

October

Teresa Hooley

Praised be my Lord for Brother October,
Who is exceedingly forthright,
Tempestuous and loud.
He coloreth the woods with glory,
So that they burn and glow.
He raketh them with his winds
And the leaves are scattered abroad like ashes.

Thanks be to my Lord for Brother October.
The plough worketh beside him,
And the earth is furrowed for the sowing of bread.
Beauty followeth after
In a cloud of wings,
For man doth not live by bread alone.
Brother rook plundereth the walnut-tree
And Sister squirrel the hazel;
Brother thrush pulleth the berries of the yew,
For your heavenly Father feedeth them.

Praised be my Lord for Brother October,
Tenth of the apostle months of the circling year.

122

Memorandum to Saint Francis—April 16

Sister Mary Francis, P.C.

Because a curious dream ruined your heart
And your ambitions melted into songs,
We shall all take up candles
Today, and love like clouds.

The day Christ gashed your hands and feet and side,
We stirred in deep folds of eternity;
And down some secret avenue of Being,
Our uncreated voices called you: Father!

We rouse the night with antiphons, and blame
Our sleep with psalmody. Because you wept
Your own eyes pure as blindness, we shall keep
An everlasting vigil of your dreams,

Intruding on your glory for a witness
How, when you dragged protesting stones one season,
Talking of ladies and of holy living,
Our cloister sprang up on the floor of Heaven.

What unremembered bird, I wonder, listened
Down seven centuries the day your vows
Robbed Lucifer's throne of loneliness, and heard us
Singing, by rumor, here among these trees!

Children of Francis: 1953

Sister Mary Francis, P.C.

Where shall a diaphanous dream find spaces
For drifting now, I wonder, when the thoughts
Of men leap up like tenements, and commerce
Hawks cruel canticle down every street?

The treaty-tables smirk like chromium
Where lands of paunch and pinstripes prate of peace.
The vases of the universe are brightly
Jammed with paper flowers, and the old songs

Roll like tears down liberation's drains.
Still, in the bustling forums, sandalled strangers
Threaten the bombers with their: *Pax et bonum!*
And wilt some cannons with a Canticle.

Who shall devise a torture to defeat them?—
These men whose Father's hands and feet were torn!
What clever engineer shall murder singing
Out of the Seraph's daughters in their cloister?

The ancient smile of Francis arches over
Buckets of anxious sand at every door,
The waiting hoses, and the triple-chamber
For rinsing poisons from the bewildered air.

Learn new prostrations gay humility never
Dreamed of (on stomach, not on heart), poor world,
Not guessing how you roll in all your worried
Quick convolutions in the Hand of God.

But let the heirs of an incredible vision
Heavy with Francis' dreams, light with his songs,
Keep their fantastic certainties for glowing
Candles in the sucking swamps of fear.

And still, in the bustling forums, sandalled strangers
Threaten the bombers with their: *Pax et bonum!*
Wilting the cannons with a Canticle.

Epitaph

Sister Mary Francis, P.C.

Here lies the ideal of Saint Francis:
Pressed in the folds of earth, the little plant,
Drooped to a smile of meager flesh and bone.

Here lies the triumph of the little poor man,
The lovely, wasted witness to his dream.
Bring no polite compassion to her coffin
And stay the pitying upward flight of brow
For Francis and his dream without a haven,
His mad, impossible schemes. Here lies the proof
His dream was wholly possible to her heart.

Here lies the refutation for crawling cautions,
Sweet, mute rebuttal to any compromise.
Her crypt is full of flower-talk, and gladly
The stars come swimming down to kiss her face
Caught in its quiet splendor. Be still! Be still!
The place is full of angel-talk or song.

Here lies the fragile flower of Saint Francis
Stronger than armies! Here, the unswerving gaze
Shuttered at last on earth and turned on Godhead.

Here lies the testimony to Saint Francis:
Clare of Assisi.

                    Who weeps, weep but for joy.

Genealogy

Sister Mary Francis, P.C.

In those days, Francis smiled a revolution,
And all the rusted spearpoints of the Gospel
Shot on complacency. The world was wounded
Straight through its satisfaction. He begot
A generation of nomads set to wander
Across the earth like songs, and drift to heaven.

He had a daughter, Clare, who lost her heart
Entirely to a Lover Who solemnly promised
Her nothing on earth, and Paradise thereafter.

And she was barren, as the courteous sun
That lends its fire to moon and stars, reserving
Its burning glory whole, is brightly barren.
Barren as plainsong seeding the soul with hunger
For heaven, barren as innocence of skies
That roof whole, sinning worlds with vast compassion,
Barren by splendid vow, was the virgin Clare.

These are the children of her barrenness:
Singers who shatter the patient night's repose
With thunderclaps of psalms, startle the day
With songs like sudden lilacs—cloistered deep
In niches of the cathedraled universe.

In their generation, who will number
The daughters of the barrenness of Clare,
Pouring their lives like smiling waters into
The world's dry riverbeds? Now, in the census
Of seven hundred years, write: She begot
Each of these virgins in these secret cloisters
And all who keep vigil beneath some layers of earth
For the glad final count. Let the virgin's daughters
Rise up and call her, Mother! Thanks be to God.

Saint Francis Sings a New Song

Imogen Clark

Saint Francis, lover of laughter,
Paused on the road that led to town,
And keen eyes, peering from the wood,
Saw him in the sunlight there
Gird up his woolen gown.
Gay as a troubadour he stood,
One rod close-cupped against his chin,
As though it were a violin;
And back and forth across his arm
He drew his staff, a fiddler's bow,
Weaving a sorcerer's charm,
Luring a little tune to grow. . . .
Almost the listening air
Could hear faint music trailing after
Like bells of silver swung
Now high . . . now low. . . .
And oh, the way Saint Francis sang!
The bending blue with rapture rang.
Yet, full of wonder, friars and birds
Hearkened to all those unknown words
That lightly tripped as in a dance—

Not Latin, nor their own loved tongue,
But flower-winged from France,
As up, and up, the new song soared
To lay its gold before the Lord.

Paradox

Sister Maryanna, O.P.

Saint Francis loved the Lady Poverty—
Mere earthly wealth did this Poor Man despise.
But can one call him poor? Reflect that he
For jewel-coffer had the star-strewn skies,
For lamp to guide his steps, the lucent moon;
The choral chant he sang with wildwood birds:
"Praise God, my little brothers. Keep in tune!"
In rose leaf and in rocks he read God's words.
The wide world was his cloister, and his cell
Had but the far horizon for its wall.
This Poverello chose his treasure well—
He whom we rich folk Little Poor Man call.
    From Umbrian sunsets Francis minted gold,
    Rejoicing in his Master's hundredfold.

Franciscans

Hyacinth Blocker, O.F.M.

We are the singing troubadours of God,
His minstrels to a world in need of song,
What though we track the footprints Christ has trod
And feel with Him a false world's lashing thong,
If still—like Him—recalling not its wrong,
We journey on, full pleased to bear the rod,
Content to burn our lives away in song—
His playthings, minstrels, singing fools of God!

And for our pay we ask no worldly boon,
We crave no other recompense than this:
That flinging music as we march along
And scattering light to men in sin's abyss,
Forgetting us—as men forget—full soon,
You still remember down the years our song.

The Wooing of Saint Francis

Hyacinth Blocker, O.F.M.

I woo unseen, this groaning winter's night,
Within my cell
(And it is well),
For here, cramped in by four bare walls, I plight
My troth to Lady Poverty,
Free from that frenzied ecstasy
Of passion gripping lovers in the world,
And their remorse when morning skies unfurled
Leave tears of salt where pungent kisses burned
The night before . . .
I need no more
Such lover's love to quench my wild heart's fire,
Nor crave I more the surges of desire
For woman's beauty . . . I have learned
To value less
Such bitterness
Since Poverty has pressed her shrunken lips
To mine.
One kiss enough to be apocalypse
Divine!

The Wolf of Gubbio

Hyacinth Blocker, O.F.M.

No massive locks
Could shield their flocks
From this fierce prowling foe,
Nor baited lure
Hope to secure
The wolf of Gubbio.

Unconquerable,
No force could quell
His ravages or tame,
Until one day
Across his way
God's Little Poor Man came.

The gentle Saint
Thus made complaint:
"Dear Brother Wolf, my friend,
These raids must cease;
Come, live in peace,
And for your sins amend."

Then peasant saw,
In wondering awe,
The wild wolf acquiescing,
And like a lamb
Beside its dam
Kneel down for Francis' blessing . . .

If you could thus
This barbarous
Wild wolf make so benign,
Ah, Francis, tame,
And quench the flame
In this wild heart of mine!

Saint Francis and the Cloud

Marie De L. Welch

"Forget all creatures that ever God made . . . with
a seemly recklessness take no heed of them. . . . As
this *cloud of unknowing* is betwixt thee and thy
God, so put a *cloud of forgetting* betwixt thee and all
creatures."—THE CLOUD OF UNKNOWING.

With such unseemly caution have I taken heed
That now, if I stand, if I run, if I lie down,
Awake in my speaking, asleep in my dreaming
     prayers,
I must remember.

I kneel as the birds bend wing.

In my sleep the lamb in his aureole of wool,
The lion in the halo of his mane,
Ramble together like God's works, my dream.

How can I not remember when I run
The rapid wind, the spaces of His voice;
The rock, His depths of silence, when I stand;
When I break bread, the heavens of His crumbs?

All things remind me:
All bones of angels,
All fires of grass,
All ashes of the sun.

How can I forget the rays of light in the light,
Or the roots in darkness, or myself
In the dust, in the air their mingling?

I forget nothing. I am unseemly.

All these distractions in the loves of God,
The action of these dreams between His works,
Amuse God's lovers in their love of God.

But how shall I alone put on the cloud
And love Him not in works, His works of love,
But all unknowing love only His being?

I am not worthy. All things remind me:
All tombs of shells,
All clay of birth,
All sorrow of green vines.

Most heedful of His Works, I am least use.
Most careful of His loves, I am most cold.

Most knowing of His creatures, I am lost.

And yet I am unknowing—of despair.

All things remind me:
All is generous.

The beast that knows a little less than I
Clothes in his little mist my naked care
And being hid in the more reckless bird
The bird in the most seemly recklessness
Is held, is hidden, in the crumb of bread.

And all things clouding, sky by deeper sky,
Brother by worthier brother, I may come
To all unknowing that is Loving God.

To Saint Francis

A. Babington Smith

St. Francis, who were ever friend
   Of overdriven man and beast,
On this and every day extend
   Your blessing unto these, our least:

The starving dog, the alley-cat,
   Who have no friendly food-dish shelf,
Provide for these, remembering that
   You begged for scraps of food yourself;

Please bless the gray-faced cart-horse, too,
   Patiently breathing fumes of gas,
Bring him to fields he never knew
   (You named your body "Brother Ass")—

Fulfill each hunted creature's needs:
   The cornered deer with pleading eye—
The wingèd duck crawling in the reeds—
   Bless him, and let him quickly die;

Friend of all friendless things, we ask
   To live our lives upon your plan—
Teach us your even harder task—
   Teach us to love our fellow man!

The Saint

Humbert Wolfe

Saint Francis of Assisi, do you remember
   the sacred mountain, green above the lake,
where first the vines and then the olives clamber,
   and the flowers, so lulled with beauty, never
      wake——
                  gold, crimson, blue,
   on the long drowsy terraces you loved and knew?

Still in the lake the painted island town
   to the brown shelter of its Minster creeps,
and still the kerchiefed boatman, bending down,
   scarce stirs the burnished water with his sweeps,
               and from the hill
   the monastery bells affirm your gospel still.

Your gospel of the birds and of the flowers,
   how every petal God has deigned to paint
has by its mere enamel all the powers,
   and more than all the beauty of the saint,
             and how the swallow
   worships with arrow-flight that prayer is fain to
      follow.

140

Your gospel of acceptance, that transposes
    God, and this earthly beauty He has made,
finding the resurrection in the roses
    and all the angels in a single blade,
                              and having heard
    the twelve Apostles in the voice of a bird.

And, as with beauty, so with ugliness,
    asking the mire that your feet had trod
with its long patience, to redeem and bless
    the soul's impatience, when the feet of God
                              pass by, as though
    He cared not what He crushed, and did not even
    know.

With ugliness, or what so seemed, and sin
    that is no more than beauty's other side,
your gospel, like your Master, entered in
    and by acceptance proved what sin denied—
                              that wickedness
    is part of the soul of God, and calls to Him no less.

You sought no cloister, but the rose-white briar
    of perfect understanding and its pardon
built walls, that shut out envy, hate, desire,
    or changed them into flowers in your garden,
                              since all were part
    of the burden of man, and therefore of your heart.

Still on your sacred mountain the cold lances
    of the moon ring the target of your mere,
and while one man loves birds and flowers, Saint
    Francis,
    you and the company of saints are here,
                    while one man knows
    that all creation is simple as a rose,

Fades like a rose, and has the rose's thorn,
    but sees behind the fallen petal the bud,
and understands, although his heart is torn,
    there was and is salvation in blood—
                    while anyone
    lies down to sleep, accepting everything beneath
    the sun.

Saint Francis of Assisi

Harry F. Leary

Take all; take all; take everything
The world can give to me.
I'll still be rich with my true love,
My Lady Poverty.

My ragged cloak and sturdy staff—
The crusts men give to me
Are all I want, that I may serve
My Lady Poverty.

Compassion for the beggar's plight
Is not enough to free
My shackled soul; I must embrace
My Lady Poverty.

Christ had not where to lay His Head—
My hearth and home must be
What chills the body, warms the soul—
My Lady Poverty.

No coin may lie within my purse—
Nay, no purse may mine be.
My only wealth be Christ's own wealth—
My Lady Poverty.

I'd Know You!

Rose Mazan

If . . . by chance . . . we should meet—
You'd be walking down the street—
> I'd know you!

Not by the clothes that you'd wear,
Nor by the color of your hair . . .
> I'd know you!

By your kindness to rich and poor,
By your joyous spirit . . . sure!
> I'd know you!

How you'd be followed by man and beast,
And how you'd look—when you met a priest . . .
> I'd know you!

Tho' the wounds in your hands and feet were hid,
I'd know you by what you said and did!
> I'd know you!

O Father Francis . . . we did meet!
In another's shoes, you walked our street—
> I knew you!

144

I was worn and tired and feeling blue,
You only smiled, but it warmed me through.

                              I knew you!

Here are *my* shoes, dear Poor Little Man,
Let them carry you where'er they can . . .

                              I beg you!

You can lead more men to God,
As in my shoes this earth you trod,

                        And bless you!

Saint Francis of Assisi

Pierson Ricks

What ragged beggar stalks the dusty road,
His gaunt face scrawled with phrases of privation,
His thin back bent as by a phantom load,
His weary belly ever on vacation?

Who is this wretch, and why should he rejoice,
Yet have no comfort jingling in his purse?
Why praise his God, and lift aloud his voice,
When every godly notice seems a curse?

This man is Francis, humbly greet him back,
For angels tip-toe by him on the track.

Medallion of Saint Francis

Harry Elmore Hurd

A craftsman, loving beauty, cut rare glass
To fit his dream. Old blues, and orange-brown,
Portrayed Saint Francis in a leaded gown
As plain as poverty. The slow sands pass
Unnoticed through life's fragile hour-glass,
While new Assisians, watching Youth cast down
His clothes, renouncing Wealth, call Francis "Clown!
Cracked brained! Close relative of stubborn ass!"

Wild brother wolf and sister flowers nod,
Sleek silvery fishes shake with shining glee,
And gabby sparrows listen reverently
To tales of him who loved the earth like God.
Mankind lays golden love upon the grave
Of him who served his fellows like a slave.

Francis of Assisi

Bertha Gerneaux Woods

Shy, woodland creatures perched upon your shoulders:
Brother you were to all the outdoor things—
Small, creeping insects hidden under boulders—
Over your head the whir of flashing wings.

Meeting the winter's icy blasts unshrinking,
Wrapped in those tattered garments gladly worn,
Taking the leper in your arms, and thinking
Yours a high privilege to brave men's scorn.

Up the steep mountain, heedless of derision,
Forty days' fast, the world's good reckoned loss;
Then, to your startled eyes, that Seraph Vision
Nailed like your Lord and Master to a cross.

What were the ecstasy and pain that shook you!
"Lord, Lord, the *meaning?* Make me understand."
Swift on your flesh the answer overtook you:
Jesus' own wound-prints stamped on either hand.

Ah, had it come—that likeness to your Master?
What the strange thing—a spear-thrust in your side?
Memoried words make weakened heart-beats faster?
"When I awake. . . . I shall be satisfied."

Shaken with awe and solemn exaltation,
Down the mount's slope you went with trembling
    feet.
Almost was ended now earth's hard probation.
Surely you knew it—found the knowledge sweet?

Saint Francis

Gertrude Huntington McGiffert

Deep in the heart of a primal wood
  Where nobody goes,
  Which nobody knows,
Saint Francis was talking with bird and beast
Bidding them pray before they feast.
You could hear steps padding from far, from near,
As the lesser folk gathered—a truce to fear.
The birds were all there and the beasts of the wood,
Savage wolves kneeled, the forest trees stood,
Eagle and dove Saint Francis fed,
A friendly lion made warm his bed.
The watchful hawk he held to his breast;
The frolicsome lambs he loved the best.
With Lady Poverty, starved had he,
And humble he was, as a child may be,
But starved and humble he cherished them all,
As year by year they came at his call.
  Deep in the heart of a primal wood
    Where nobody goes,
    Which nobody knows.

At midnight all a circle made,
Saint Francis preached and none was afraid.
He told them gently God's command,
A little green adder asleep on his hand.
He taught his yearning kindred there
That one and all were the Father's care,
Taught them their nature to defy
And put all savage instincts by.
In shame that night the brown bear hid,
Filled with remorse for the things he did.

   Deep in the heart of a primal wood
       Where nobody goes,
       Which nobody knows.

Brother Wind, Brother Water, the Flowers, the Sod,
He commended all for their joy in God,
Right gladsome saluted mother earth,
To charity urged them, to mercy and mirth,
To plead for pardon, love and grace—
Each prayed and praised, and bowed his face.
When his sisters, the Stars, paled one by one,
All sang his Canticle to the Sun.
Then birds and beasts slipped off and away
And Saint Francis was left alone to pray.

   Deep in the heart of a primal wood
       Where nobody goes,
       Which nobody knows.

Dedication to My Gray Lady

Fra Jerome, T.O.R.

She is gray but beautiful; lovely as the beggar-maid
of King Cophetua.

She is clothed in patched sackcloth of the color of
ashes, with a girdle of rope; but the scent of her
garments is as the odor of frankincense.

The wolf lies at her door and she shares her hearth-
cake with him.

My Gray Lady was at Bethlehem and Nazareth; a
faithful handmaid of The Little Mother, most
Blessed of all Ladies.

Barefooted she comes leaping across the holy mountains: Hermon and Carmel; Tabor and Olivet;
Quarantina and Calvary. Rivers of tears shed she
weeping under a Tree.

Mourning she went through all the land until she
came to Umbria: there the Little Poor Man
espoused her.

Many sing the praises of her beauty in fair poetry and
lovely paintings but list not where to find her.
Where does she dwell?

Veiled in the gray mist down by The River; alone in
a little thatched hut of wattle and daub, swept
by cold winds and rains. There too would I seek
her and walk with her. What can I bring her?

Torch-wood and cassava and golden corncobs.

O! Let me but sweep the threshold of her door!

From The Death of Saint Francis

Marion A. Habig, O.F.M.

From the Spanish in the Church at Guanabacoa, Cuba

His death began the day the stigmata
Made him a living replica of Christ;
As Jesus dies while hanging on the Cross,
On Verna's height was Francis crucified.
And at his passing there was present too
The good and pious matron Giacoma,
Who by her weeping and her sorrowing
Another mourner sought to emulate;
For dying Francis close resembled Christ,
And Giacoma was like to Magdalene.

Prayer to St. Francis

Frances Frost

Will there come a day
when the fox, at bay,
may find man's shoulder
his shelter, his boulder?

When will the deer
stand without fear
while man's hand touches
his russet haunches?

When will the snare
return to air
the bright-winged captive
to praise God and live?

St. Francis, when will
man cease to kill
the shy, and that other—
his shyer brother?

A Christmass Carol for Saint Francis' Ears

Raymond E. F. Larsson

Wolves in dim the forest prowl,
　　Birds that dream by night,
Foxes in thy lairs, and fowl,
　　Praise ye now *The Light:*

Lo, the lion shall lie down,
　　Lamb be mighty *King,*
Wrath be merry, Hate not frown,
　　Praising *Christ,* shall sing.

Lizards, moles, ye stoats and mules,
　　Larks and all ye kine,
Knaves and wisemen, all ye fools,
　　All ye snorting swine;

Nightingale and asp and hen,
　　Cloud and fire, stone,
Praise ye; praise, ye worlds and men,
　　Christ The Light and *One.*

Snow, ye windy blasts, be still:
    Hush!—here's mightier *Breath,*
Calmeth wrath to *His Meek Will:*
    Yea, rebuketh Death.

Darks and ages, see, adore:
    Christ the Lord is born,
Lord of Earth and *Heaven's Lord*
    Lights all suns' first morn—

Light of Suns and *Light of Souls,*
    Light of worlds shall be.
Praise!—our ash shall burn as coals
    Praised the more be *He!*

God's Little Creatures: Foreword

Joaquin Antonio Peñalosa
From the Spanish by Arthur Train, Jr.

And the other creatures on the face of the earth are made for man, to help him achieve the end for which he was created. . . .

Even God's little beasts—O Francis! O Ignatius!—can help us dominate and regulate our life and our poetry.

Now, in Paradise, they are a part of history human and divine, from the clever serpent to the horse of the Apocalypse.

And it is the Lamb—of God—who ransoms the sins of the world.

Lament for a Dead Burro

This was no cargo of roses, nor charcoal, nor wood on his back. Death alone was the load.

Drinking-in the moonlight, he had come along the
  trail;

158

but over his eyes there passed a shadowy veil.
   It was his last haul.

They brought alcohol, ran for the doctor,
     as the heart dreamed on;
but the children's anguished kisses told us
     our Brother was already gone.

No idle epitaph for him, no funeral, first class;
leave him to die where he slept, in the dry grass.

And may the small green birds that climb his mane
let him sleep sound; he will not wake again.

May his flesh be whipped by the winds, and by the
     sun dried,
till his deserted bones are like hacked-off limbs
     of an old white tree that has died.

Did pain strike? Was he just old and spent?
Let none ask. Let no death notices be sent;
let no wreaths be piled to mark where the corpse lies.
A cross and a star in the night skies
suffice.

For the little white donkey of the pageants of
     Christmastide,

for the little black Palm Sunday donkey that Christ
    did ride,
let the burro drivers go saddle a star.
You, stay where you are!

Our shoulders, too, grow stiff beneath life's load
of death, with Mystery the goad.

Earth calls us. Let him die! But breathe a tear
first, a plaint, into this furry ear.
Earth calls. All dies, but from the dead dust
Spring will rise.

Sermon to the Fishes

Beloved Brothers in Our Lord Jesus Christ:

    In the name of the Father, who is your Creator,
    and Archangel Raphael, fisherman and world
        navigator,

    Keep your round eyes still—still with the soul's
        peace;
    cross yourselves and listen till my story cease. . . .

Lowly sardine, your salty ocean nook
outvies the sweet waters of any pond or brook.

Do not be curious, minnow, to see the world;
land is a prison; sea's borders are never furled. . . .

Rower and rowboat in one, go seek, O Fish,
the crystal Paradise you received in Genesis.

Stigmata

A. M. Sullivan

Francis rode to battle in the armor of a knight,
He rode upon an Arab steed whose hooves set stone
aflame,
But Francis was in tatters when he put his pride to
flight
And Francis rode a donkey when a leper called his
name.

Francis kissed a leper's sores, he ate a leper's meal
And a thousand men with leprous souls came asking
to be clean.
The nobles met him in the street, the vagrant dogged
his heel
And everywhere his sandal touched the withered path
was green.

Francis loved the things of earth that served the King
of Heaven,
The wings of birds, the wings of words upon the
gentle breeze,
He preached in singing parables to knave and bawd
and craven
Till duke and churl and sundry beasts came down
upon their knees.

Francis was a little man who chiseled the mountain
  bone
For choir, nave and belfry on Damian's crooked stair.
Sin wrapped a heart of adamant within the heavy
  stone
But Francis cracked it open with the cudgeling of
  prayer.

Francis climbed up Calvary to shame the Saracen;
(Mahomet's crescent dimmed the sun, and blood was
  on his sword)
But Francis took the burning cross on Mount Alverno
  when
He felt the nails in hands and feet pressed by the
  living Lord.

Poor he was, and proud he was, when the Saviour
  bade him go
With a happy burden on his back and Simons, young
  and strong,
To share the weight, to share the pain, and all the
  world to know
How much of love spilled from his heart, and filled
  the sky with song.

LIST OF POETS

LIST OF POETS